I0883273

Addendum I
to
AMMO & BALLISTICS 4

Changes to *Ammo & Ballistics 4* for the Year 2010

by
Bob Forker

SAFARI PRESS

Addendum I to Ammo & Ballistics 4 for the Year 2010 © 2010 by Robert Forker. All rights reserved. No part of this publication may be used or reproduced in any form or by any means without permission from the publisher.

The trademark Safari Press ® is registered with the U.S. Patent and Trademark Office and with government trademark and patent offices in other countries.

Forker, Robert

Addendum to the fourth edition

Safari Press Inc.

2010, Long Beach, California

ISBN 978-1-57157-357-5

Library of Congress Catalog Card Number: 2010926808

10 9 8 7 6 5 4 3 2 1

Printed in the United States of America

Readers wishing to receive the Safari Press catalog, featuring many fine books on big-game hunting, wingshooting, and sporting firearms, should write to Safari Press Inc., P.O. Box 3095, Long Beach, CA 90803, U.S.A. Tel: (714) 894-9080 or visit our Web site at www.safaripress.com.

Changes to A&B4 for the year 2010

Most ammunition manufacturers are constantly changing individual elements of their product lines. They do this for a variety of reasons such as the availability of components, a decision to add a new caliber or bullet weight, or simply because a particular listing isn't selling well enough to justify further production. In order to keep *Ammo & Ballistics* as up to date as possible, Safari Press is now publishing a list of changes to cover any ammendments made since *A&B4* was printed.

This list doesn't really stand alone. It is a supplement to the listings shown in *A&B4* . The reader is urged to consult the listings in *A&B4* and then the changes listed here. Only additions or changes in the performance of a particular stock number are shown here. Some listings shown in *A&B4* have been discontinued by the manufacturer since the book was published. Because the products can remain on dealer's shelves for several years, the discontinued items are not listed as changes here.

There are a couple of significant developments in the ammunition business since *A&B4* was printed. The holding company for PMC has changed, although most of the specifications for the PMC product line remain unchanged. Magtech has merged with Sellier & Bellot. It appears from their current catalog that Sellier & Bellot will eventually concentrate on rifle ammunition while the Magtech label will be used for handgun ammunition. This conversion, if that is what it is, is not complete at this time, and there are some listings by Sellier & Bellot for handgun ammunition. Most of these listings have been assigned new stock numbers.

Finally, since *A&B4* was printed, there has been a greater emphasis on lead-free bullets. We have marked the lead free ammunition listings with the symbol ☺ to make them easy to recognize.

Data for Small and Medium Centerfire Rifle Cartridges

.204 Ruger

Cor-Bon 26-grain Varmint Grenade (SD20426VG/20) ☺

G1 Ballistic Coefficient = 0.100

Distance • Yards	Muzzle	100	200	300	400	500	600	800	1000
Velocity • fps	4200	3070	2179	1469	1046	872	760	592	463
Energy • ft-lbs	1019	544	274	125	63	44	33	20	12
Taylor KO Index	3.2	2.3	1.7	1.1	0.8	0.7	0.6	0.4	0.3
Path • Inches	-1.5	+1.2	0.0	-8.9	-34.6	-91.8	-194.8	-599.9	-1413
Wind Drift • Inches	0.0	2.2	10.0	27.1	58.0	101.1	153.6	286.8	465.2

Hornady 30-grain NTX (83209) ☺

G1 Ballistic Coefficient = 0.205

Distance • Yards	Muzzle	100	200	300	400	500	600	800	1000
Velocity • fps	4225	3632	3114	2652	2234	1856	1525	1077	892
Energy • ft-lbs	1189	879	646	468	332	230	155	77	53
Taylor KO Index	3.7	3.2	2.7	2.3	2.0	1.6	1.3	0.9	0.8
Path • Inches	-1.5	+0.6	0.0	-4.2	-13.4	-29.6	-56.1	-161.3	-385.5
Wind Drift - Inches	0.0	1.1	4.7	11.4	22.0	37.8	60.5	129.5	222.5

Federal 32-grain Speer TNT Green (P204D) ☺

G1 Ballistic Coefficient = 0.160

Distance • Yards	Muzzle	100	200	300	400	500	600	800	1000
Velocity • fps	4030	3320	2710	2170	1710	1330	1077	855	724
Energy • ft-lbs	1155	980	520	335	205	125	82	52	37
Taylor KO Index	3.8	3.1	2.5	2.0	1.6	1.2	1.0	0.8	0.7
Path • Inches	-1.5	+0.9	0.0	-5.7	-19.1	-45.3	-89.8	-279.4	-659.8
Wind Drift • Inches	0.0	1.4	5.9	14.6	23.9	51.1	82.6	167.9	276.5

.22 Hornet

Federal 30-grain Speer TNT Green (P22D) ☺

G1 Ballistic Coefficient = 0.091

Distance • Yards	Muzzle	100	200	300	400	500	600	800	1000
Velocity • fps	3150	2150	1390	990	830	720	628	479	365
Energy • ft-lbs	660	310	130	65	45	35	26	15	9
Taylor KO Index	3.0	2.1	1.3	1.0	0.8	0.7	0.6	0.5	0.4
Path • Inches	-1.5	+3.3	0.0	-22.8	-78.7	-179.7	-358.6	-1002	-2278
Wind Drift • Inches	0.0	3.5	17.2	46.2	87.9	139.4	201.3	361.7	585.8

Hornady 32-grain V-MAX (8302)

G1 Ballistic Coefficient = 0.109

Distance • Yards	Muzzle	100	200	300	400	500	600	800	1000
Velocity • fps	3070	2246	1571	1116	919	803	712	568	454
Energy • ft-lbs	732	392	192	97	66	50	39	25	16
Taylor KO Index	3.4	2.5	1.8	1.2	1.0	0.9	0.8	0.6	0.5
Path • Inches	-1.5	+2.9	0.0	-17.6	-62.9	-149.3	-290.0	-795.7	-1744
Wind Drift • Inches	0.0	2.9	13.9	37.1	72.6	117.1	169.9	302.4	478.3

Sellier & Bellot 45-grain SP (V330012U)

G1 Ballistic Coefficient = 0.124

Distance • Yards	Muzzle	100	200	300	400	500	600	800	1000
Velocity • fps	2346	1726	1251	998	869	777	701	575	473
Energy • ft-lbs	550	298	157	99	76	60	49	33	22
Taylor KO Index	3.4	2.5	1.8	1.4	1.3	1.1	1.0	0.8	0.7
Path • Inches	-1.5	+5.3	0.0	-27.7	-90.2	-198.7	-365.0	-927.1	-1920
Wind Drift • Inches	0.0	3.8	17.4	42.8	77.3	119.2	168.3	290.6	450.4

Sellier & Bellot 45-grain FMJ (V330002U)

G1 Ballistic Coefficient = 0.124

Distance • Yards	Muzzle	100	200	300	400	500	600	800	1000
Velocity • fps	2346	1726	1251	998	869	777	701	575	473
Energy • ft-lbs	550	298	157	99	76	60	49	33	22
Taylor KO Index	3.4	2.5	1.8	1.4	1.3	1.1	1.0	0.8	0.7
Path • Inches	-1.5	+5.3	0.0	-27.7	-90.2	-198.7	-365.0	-927.1	-1920
Wind Drift • Inches	0.0	3.8	17.4	42.8	77.3	119.2	168.3	290.6	450.4

.222 Remington

Sellier & Bellot 50-grain SP (V330122U)

G1 Ballistic Coefficient = 0.248

Distance • Yards	Muzzle	100	200	300	400	500	600	800	1000
Velocity • fps	3215	2821	2460	2127	1821	1548	1317	948	888
Energy • ft-lbs	1148	884	672	502	368	266	193	117	88
Taylor KO Index	5.1	4.5	3.9	3.4	2.9	2.5	2.1	1.5	1.4
Path • Inches	-1.5	+1.4	0.0	-7.2	-22.2	-47.8	-88.0	-235.4	-513.9
Wind Drift • Inches	0.0	1.1	4.7	11.4	21.8	36.9	57.5	116.8	195.3

Norma 50-grain Soft Point (15711)

G1 Ballistic Coefficient = 0.185

Distance • Yards	Muzzle	100	200	300	400	500	600	800	1000
Velocity • fps	3199	2679	2215	1800	1449	1181	1019	848	734
Energy • ft-lbs	1136	797	545	360	233	155	115	80	60
Taylor KO Index	5.1	4.3	3.5	2.9	2.4	1.9	1.6	1.4	1.2
Path • Inches	-1.5	+1.6	0.0	-8.9	-28.6	-65.2	-126.6	-357.3	-782.3
Wind Drift • Inches	0.0	1.5	6.7	16.6	32.8	56.9	88.8	170.4	271.7

Federal 50-grain Soft Point (222A)

G1 Ballistic Coefficient = 0.223

Distance • Yards	Muzzle	100	200	300	400	500	600	800	1000
Velocity • fps	3140	2710	2320	1960	1640	1370	1163	943	823
Energy • ft-lbs	1095	815	595	425	300	205	150	99	75
Taylor KO Index	5.0	4.3	3.7	3.1	2.6	2.2	1.9	1.5	1.3
Path • Inches	-1.5	+1.6	0.0	-8.2	-25.7	-56.5	-104.6	-286.6	-624.7
Wind Drift • Inches	0.0	1.3	5.5	13.4	26.0	44.4	69.6	138.2	225.0

Norma 50-grain Full Jacket (15715)

G1 Ballistic Coefficient = 0.192

Distance • Yards	Muzzle	100	200	300	400	500	600	800	1000
Velocity • fps	3199	2697	2247	1843	1496	1222	1047	868	753
Energy • ft-lbs	1136	809	562	378	249	166	122	84	63
Taylor KO Index	5.1	4.3	3.6	2.9	2.4	2.0	1.7	1.4	1.2
Path • Inches	-1.5	+1.6	0.0	-8.6	-27.6	-62.4	-120.4	-339.0	-742.8
Wind Drift • Inches	0.0	1.5	6.4	15.9	31.1	53.8	84.3	163.1	261.3

Lapua 55-grain FMJ (4315020)

G1 Ballistic Coefficient = 0.192

Distance • Yards	Muzzle	100	200	300	400	500	600	800	1000
Velocity • fps	2885	2522	2188	1880	1603	1365	1178	967	851
Energy • ft-lbs	1016	777	584	431	314	228	169	114	88
Taylor KO Index	5.1	4.4	3.9	3.3	2.8	2.4	2.1	1.7	1.5
Path • Inches	-1.5	+2.0	0.0	-9.3	-28.6	-61.4	-113.1	-297.9	-631.2
Wind Drift • Inches	0.0	1.3	5.4	13.2	25.3	42.7	66.2	129.8	210.7

.223 Remington

Winchester 36-grain Ballistic Silvertip (S22336RLF) ☺

G1 Ballistic Coefficient = 0.201

Distance • Yards	Muzzle	100	200	300	400	500	600	800	1000
Velocity • fps	3800	3251	2766	2330	1935	1586	1300	981	836
Energy • ft-lbs	1110	813	588	417	287	193	131	75	54
Taylor KO Index	4.3	3.6	3.1	2.6	2.2	1.8	1.5	1.1	0.9
Path • Inches	-1.5	+0.9	0.0	-5.5	-17.5	-38.9	-73.4	-215.1	-499.9
Wind Drift • Inches	0.0	1.1	4.9	11.8	22.7	39.0	62.0	129.7	219.2

Cor-Bon 36-grain Varmint Grenade (SD22336VG/20) ☺

G1 Ballistic Coefficient = 0.149

Distance • Yards	Muzzle	100	200	300	400	500	600	800	1000
Velocity • fps	3600	2907	2311	1791	1366	1086	942	774	654
Energy • ft-lbs	1036	676	427	256	149	94	71	48	34
Taylor KO Index	4.1	3.3	2.7	2.1	1.6	1.3	1.1	0.9	0.8
Path • Inches	-1.5	+1.3	0.0	-8.0	-27.2	-65.2	-132.6	-394.2	-890.4
Wind Drift • Inches	0.0	1.7	7.4	18.7	37.9	67.0	104.9	200.1	320.0

Fiocchi 40-grain Hornady V-MAX Polymer Tip (223HVB)

G1 Ballistic Coefficient = 0.200

Distance • Yards	Muzzle	100	200	300	400	500	600	800	1000
Velocity • fps	3650	3117	2644	2217	1832	1497	1232	954	818
Energy • ft-lbs	1183	862	620	436	298	199	135	81	60
Taylor KO Index	4.7	4.0	3.4	2.8	2.3	1.9	1.6	1.2	1.0
Path • Inches	-1.5	+1.1	0.0	-6.1	-19.3	-43.1	-82.5	-238.3	-454.0
Wind Drift • Inches	0.0	1.2	5.1	12.5	24.2	41.7	66.2	136.6	227.8

Remington 45-grain Jacketed Iron-Tin Core HP (DV223RA) ☺

G1 Ballistic Coefficient = 0.161

Distance • Yards	Muzzle	100	200	300	400	500	600	800	1000
Velocity • fps	3550	2911	2355	1865	1451	1150	987	811	691
Energy • ft-lbs	1251	847	554	347	210	132	97	66	48
Taylor KO Index	5.1	4.2	3.4	2.7	2.1	1.7	1.4	1.2	1.0
Path • Inches	-1.5	+1.3	0.0	-7.7	-25.6	-60.3	-121.0	-357.9	-807.5
Wind Drift • Inches	0.0	1.6	6.8	17.2	34.4	60.6	95.6	184.8	296.6

Fiocchi 45-grain Frangible Surefire (223SFNT) ☺

G1 Ballistic Coefficient = 0.142

Distance • Yards	Muzzle	100	200	300	400	500	600	800	1000
Velocity • fps	3300	2630	2050	1556	1189	991	880	729	614
Energy • ft-lbs	1067	691	419	242	141	98	77	53	38
Taylor KO Index	4.8	3.8	3.0	2.2	1.7	1.4	1.3	1.0	0.9
Path • Inches	-1.5	+1.8	0.0	-10.3	-35.3	-84.9	-169.8	-484.1	-1063
Wind Drift • Inches	0.0	1.9	8.7	22.3	45.3	78.4	119.2	219.7	346.4

Remington 50-grain AccuTip Boat Tail (PRA223RB)

G1 Ballistic Coefficient = 0.242

Distance • Yards	Muzzle	100	200	300	400	500	600	800	1000
Velocity • fps	3410	2983	2605	2252	1928	1635	1384	1052	900
Energy • ft-lbs	1291	1902	753	563	413	297	213	123	90
Taylor KO Index	5.5	4.8	4.2	3.6	3.1	2.6	2.2	1.7	1.4
Path • Inches	-1.5	+1.2	0.0	-6.4	-19.6	-42.4	-78.2	-211.2	-468.9
Wind Drift • Inches	0.0	1.1	4.5	10.8	20.7	34.9	54.6	112.5	190.8

Cor-Bon 50-grain Varmint Grenade (SD22350VG/20) ☺

G1 Ballistic Coefficient = 0.183

Distance • Yards	Muzzle	100	200	300	400	500	600	800	1000
Velocity • fps	3000	2498	2049	1652	1326	1100	972	774	654
Energy • ft-lbs	999	693	466	303	195	134	105	74	56
Taylor KO Index	4.8	4.0	3.3	2.6	2.1	1.8	1.6	1.3	1.1
Path • Inches	-1.5	+2.1	0.0	-10.5	-33.9	-77.3	-149.3	-411.2	-881.6
Wind Drift • Inches	0.0	1.7	7.4	18.6	36.7	63.1	96.8	180.8	284.6

PMC 52-grain HPBT Match (223SMA)

G1 Ballistic Coefficient = 0.251

Distance • Yards	Muzzle	100	200	300	400	500	600	800	1000
Velocity • fps	3200	2808	2447	2117	1817	1553	1324	1032	892
Energy • ft-lbs	1162	910	691	517	381	278	202	123	92
Taylor KO Index	5.3	4.7	4.1	3.5	3.0	2.6	2.2	1.7	1.5
Path • Inches	-1.5	+1.5	0.0	-7.3	-22.4	-47.9	-88.0	-234.3	-510.5
Wind Drift • Inches	0.0	1.1	4.7	11.3	21.6	36.5	56.9	115.5	193.3

Sellier & Bellot 55-grain SP (V330212U)

G1 Ballistic Coefficient = 0.260

Distance • Yards	Muzzle	100	200	300	400	500	600	800	1000
Velocity • fps	3301	2917	2565	2238	1937	1662	1422	1087	927
Energy • ft-lbs	1331	1040	804	612	458	338	247	144	105
Taylor KO Index	5.8	5.1	4.5	3.9	3.4	2.9	2.5	1.9	1.6
Path • Inches	-1.5	+1.3	0.0	-6.6	-20.2	-43.2	-78.8	-207.9	-454.0
Wind Drift • Inches	0.0	1.0	4.3	10.4	24.2	33.2	51.6	105.6	179.7

Cor-Bon 55-grain MPG (MPG22355/20) ☺

G1 Ballistic Coefficient = 0.215

Distance • Yards	Muzzle	100	200	300	400	500	600	800	1000
Velocity • fps	3300	2860	2460	2094	1782	1472	1237	976	845
Energy • ft-lbs	1330	999	739	536	379	265	187	116	87
Taylor KO Index	5.8	5.0	4.3	3.7	3.1	2.6	2.2	1.7	1.5
Path • Inches	-1.5	+1.4	0.0	-7.2	-22.4	-48.9	-91.7	-252.6	-559.1
Wind Drift • Inches	0.0	1.2	5.1	12.4	23.9	40.7	64.0	129.6	214.5

Black Hills 55-grain Barnes MPG (D223N16) ☺

G1 Ballistic Coefficient = 0.215

Distance • Yards	Muzzle	100	200	300	400	500	600	800	1000
Velocity • fps	3200	2750	2342	1971	1639	1358	1148	931	811
Energy • ft-lbs	1250	924	670	475	328	225	161	106	80
Taylor KO Index	5.6	4.8	4.1	3.5	2.9	2.4	2.0	1.6	1.4
Path • Inches	-1.5	+1.6	0.0	-8.0	-25.0	-55.1	-104.3	-288.8	-633.7
Wind Drift • Inches	0.0	1.3	5.6	13.7	26.6	45.6	71.5	142.1	231.2

Remington 55-grain AccuTip-V (PRA223RC)

G1 Ballistic Coefficient = 0.255

Distance • Yards	Muzzle	100	200	300	400	500	600	800	1000
Velocity • fps	3240	2854	2500	2172	1871	1598	1364	1054	907
Energy • ft-lbs	1282	995	763	576	427	312	227	136	100
Taylor KO Index	5.7	5.0	4.4	3.8	3.3	2.8	2.4	1.9	1.6
Path • Inches	-1.5	+1.5	0.0	-7.1	-21.7	-46.3	-84.0	-222.9	-486.2
Wind Drift • Inches	0.0	1.1	4.5	10.8	20.8	35.1	54.6	111.2	187.4

Winchester 55-grain Pointed Soft Point TIN (X223RT) ☺

G1 Ballistic Coefficient = 0.197

Distance • Yards	Muzzle	100	200	300	400	500	600	800	1000
Velocity • fps	3240	2747	2304	1905	1554	1270	1079	887	770
Energy • ft-lbs	1282	921	648	443	295	197	142	96	72
Taylor KO Index	5.7	4.8	4.1	3.4	2.7	2.2	1.9	1.6	1.4
Path • Inches	-1.5	+1.9	0.0	-8.5	-26.7	-57.6	-112.9	-318.1	-700.5
Wind Drift • Inches	0.0	1.4	6.1	15.0	29.5	50.9	80.0	156.5	252.2

Black Hills 55-grain Barnes TSX (D223N17) ☺

G1 Ballistic Coefficient = 0.210

Distance • Yards	Muzzle	100	200	300	400	500	600	800	1000
Velocity • fps	3200	2740	2324	1946	1610	1329	1125	917	798
Energy • ft-lbs	1250	917	660	463	316	216	155	103	78
Taylor KO Index	5.6	4.8	4.1	3.4	2.8	2.3	2.0	1.6	1.4
Path • Inches	-1.5	+1.6	0.0	-8.1	-25.5	-56.5	-107.3	-298.5	-655.0
Wind Drift • Inches	0.0	1.3	5.8	14.1	27.5	47.1	74.0	146.3	237.2

PMC 55-grain PSP (223B)

G1 Ballistic Coefficient = 0.264

Distance • Yards	Muzzle	100	200	300	400	500	600	800	1000
Velocity • fps	3100	2689	2314	1974	1817	1553	1333	1046	906
Energy • ft-lbs	1174	883	654	476	341	244	217	134	100
Taylor KO Index	5.5	4.7	4.1	3.5	3.2	2.7	2.3	1.8	1.6
Path • Inches	-1.5	+1.6	0.0	-7.6	-23.3	-49.6	-90.4	-237.1	-510.2
Wind Drift • Inches	0.0	1.1	4.6	11.1	21.2	35.7	55.4	112.0	187.1

Federal 55-grain Barnes Triple-Shock X-Bullet (223A) ☺

G1 Ballistic Coefficient = 0.215

Distance • Yards	Muzzle	100	200	300	400	500	600	800	1000
Velocity • fps	3200	2750	2350	1980	1650	1360	1148	931	811
Energy • ft-lbs	1250	925	670	475	330	225	161	106	80
Taylor KO Index	5.6	4.8	4.1	3.5	2.9	2.4	2.0	1.6	1.4
Path • Inches	-1.5	+1.6	0.0	-8.0	-25.1	-55.5	-104.3	-288.8	-633.7
Wind Drift • Inches	0.0	1.3	5.6	13.7	26.6	45.6	71.5	142.1	231.2

Sellier and Bellot 55-grain FMJ (223A)

G1 Ballistic Coefficient = 0.343

Distance • Yards	Muzzle	100	200	300	400	500	600	800	1000
Velocity • fps	3241	2955	2679	2423	2182	1954	1742	1376	1119
Energy • ft-lbs	1283	1064	877	717	581	466	371	231	153
Taylor KO Index	5.7	5.2	4.7	4.3	3.8	3.4	3.1	2.4	2.0
Path • Inches	-1.5	+1.2	0.0	-6.1	-18.2	-37.6	-66.1	-160.8	-329.8
Wind Drift • Inches	0.0	0.8	3.3	7.7	14.4	23.7	36.0	71.8	124.9

Fiocchi 55-grain FMJBT (223A)

G1 Ballistic Coefficient = 0.272

Distance • Yards	Muzzle	100	200	300	400	500	600	800	1000
Velocity • fps	3240	2877	2542	2231	1943	1679	1447	1110	945
Energy • ft-lbs	1281	1017	789	608	461	344	256	151	109
Taylor KO Index	5.6	4.9	4.3	3.7	3.2	2.7	2.3	1.8	1.6
Path • Inches	-1.5	+1.4	0.0	-6.8	-20.6	-43.6	-79.1	-205.6	-444.5
Wind Drift • Inches	0.0	1.0	4.2	10.1	19.2	32.1	49.7	101.3	172.7

Black Hills 55-grain Full Metal Jacket (D223N1)

G1 Ballistic Coefficient = 0.250

Distance • Yards	Muzzle	100	200	300	400	500	600	800	1000
Velocity • fps	3200	2810	2453	2123	1819	1548	1319	1029	890
Energy • ft-lbs	1250	965	735	550	404	293	213	129	97
Taylor KO Index	5.6	4.9	4.3	3.7	3.2	2.7	2.3	1.8	1.6
Path • Inches	-1.5	+1.5	0.0	-7.3	-22.4	-48.0	-88.3	-235.5	-513.3
Wind Drift • Inches	0.0	1.1	4.7	11.4	21.7	36.7	57.2	116.2	194.2

PMC 55-grain FMJ-BT (223A)

G1 Ballistic Coefficient = 0.268

Distance • Yards	Muzzle	100	200	300	400	500	600	800	1000
Velocity • fps	3200	2833	2493	2180	1893	1635	1406	1085	929
Energy • ft-lbs	1250	980	759	580	438	326	241	144	106
Taylor KO Index	5.6	5.0	4.4	3.8	3.3	2.9	2.5	1.9	1.6
Path • Inches	-1.5	+1.9	0.0	-7.1	-21.5	-45.5	-82.6	-215.8	-466.4
Wind Drift • Inches	0.0	1.1	4.7	11.4	21.7	36.7	57.2	116.2	194.2

Lapua 55-grain FMJ (4315040)

G1 Ballistic Coefficient = 0.250

Distance • Yards	Muzzle	100	200	300	400	500	600	800	1000
Velocity • fps	3130	2747	2395	2070	1770	1505	1284	1014	881
Energy • ft-lbs	1196	922	701	523	383	277	202	126	95
Taylor KO Index	5.5	4.8	4.2	3.6	3.1	2.6	2.3	1.8	1.6
Path • Inches	-1.5	+1.6	0.0	-7.7	-23.6	-50.6	-93.2	-248.2	-537.9
Wind Drift • Inches	0.0	1.1	4.9	11.7	22.5	38.0	59.2	119.3	198.0

Fusion (Federal) 62-grain Fusion (F223FS1)

G1 Ballistic Coefficient = 0.310

Distance • Yards	Muzzle	100	200	300	400	500	600	800	1000
Velocity • fps	3000	2700	2410	2150	1900	1670	1465	1151	982
Energy • ft-lbs	1240	1000	800	635	495	384	296	183	133
Taylor KO Index	6.0	5.4	4.8	4.3	3.8	3.3	2.9	2.3	1.9
Path • Inches	-1.5	+1.6	0.0	-7.7	-22.8	-48.0	-85.2	-213.7	-537.9
Wind Drift • Inches	0.0	1.0	4.1	9.6	18.2	30.3	46.4	93.2	158.1

Black Hills 62-grain Barnes TSX (D223N17) ☺

G1 Ballistic Coefficient = 0.287

Distance • Yards	Muzzle	100	200	300	400	500	600	800	1000
Velocity • fps	3100	2729	2387	2070	1780	1521	1302	1026	892
Energy • ft-lbs	1323	1026	785	590	436	318	233	145	109
Taylor KO Index	5.5	4.8	4.2	3.6	3.1	2.7	2.3	1.8	1.6
Path • Inches	-1.5	+1.6	0.0	-7.8	-23.7	-50.7	-92.8	-245.2	-528.4
Wind Drift • Inches	0.0	1.1	4.8	11.5	22.0	37.1	57.6	116.2	193.2

Cor-Bon 62-grain DPX (SD22362/20) ☺

G1 Ballistic Coefficient = 0.250

Distance • Yards	Muzzle	100	200	300	400	500	600	800	1000
Velocity • fps	2750	2397	2071	1773	1508	1286	1122	940	832
Energy • ft-lbs	1041	791	591	433	313	228	173	122	95
Taylor KO Index	5.5	4.8	4.1	3.5	3.0	2.6	2.2	1.9	1.7
Path • Inches	-1.5	+2.3	0.0	-10.5	-32.1	-69.2	-127.3	-332.5	-695.0
Wind Drift • Inches	0.0	1.4	5.9	14.2	27.4	46.1	71.1	136.5	218.0

.22-250 Remington

Winchester 35-grain Ballistic Silvertip (S22250RLF) ☺

G1 Ballistic Coefficient = 0.201

Distance • Yards	Muzzle	100	200	300	400	500	600	800	1000
Velocity • fps	4350	3729	3189	2711	2280	1890	1548	1082	891
Energy • ft-lbs	1470	1081	790	571	404	278	186	91	62
Taylor KO Index	4.9	4.2	3.6	3.0	2.6	2.1	1.7	1.2	1.0
Path • Inches	-1.5	+0.5	0.0	-4.0	-12.7	-28.2	-53.6	-155.4	-375.0
Wind Drift • Inches	0.0	1.0	4.2	10.0	19.1	32.4	51.2	109.9	194.4

Cor-Bon 36-grain Varmint Grenade (SD2225036VG/20) ☺

G1 Ballistic Coefficient = 0.149

Distance • Yards	Muzzle	100	200	300	400	500	600	800	1000
Velocity • fps	4300	3492	2815	2230	1722	1315	1059	836	701
Energy • ft-lbs	1478	975	634	398	237	138	90	56	39
Taylor KO Index	5.0	4.0	3.2	2.6	2.0	1.5	1.2	1.0	0.8
Path • Inches	-1.5	+0.7	0.0	-5.2	-17.5	-41.9	-86.6	-278.2	-670.0
Wind Drift • Inches	0.0	1.4	6.0	14.8	29.4	52.4	85.3	174.5	288.5

Remington 45-grain Jacketed Iron-Tin Core HP (DV2250RA) ☺

G1 Ballistic Coefficient = 0.161

Distance• Yards	Muzzle	100	200	300	400	500	600	800	1000
Velocity • fps	4000	3293	2690	2159	1696	1320	1076	856	725
Energy • ft-lbs	1598	1084	723	466	287	174	116	73	53
Taylor KO Index	5.8	4.7	3.9	3.1	2.4	1.9	1.5	1.2	1.0
Path • Inches	-1.5	+0.9	0.0	-5.8	-19.1	-44.8	-90.5	-280.7	-661.3
Wind Drift • Inches	0.0	1.4	5.9	14.6	29.0	51.1	82.6	167.6	275.8

Federal 50-grain Barnes Triple-Shock X-Bullet (P22250Q) ☺

G1 Ballistic Coefficient = 0.199

Distance • Yards	Muzzle	100	200	300	400	500	600	800	1000
Velocity • fps	3750	3220	2730	2290	1890	1540	1265	965	825
Energy• ft-lbs	1585	1155	830	580	395	265	178	103	76
Taylor KO Index	6.0	5.2	4.4	3.7	3.0	2.5	2.0	1.5	1.3
Path • Inches	-1.5	+0.9	0.0	-5.6	-18.0	-40.7	-77.7	-225.6	-522.1
Wind Drift • Inches	0.0	1.2	5.0	12.1	23.5	40.4	64.2	133.5	153.2

Sellier & Bellot 55-grain SBT (V330462U)

G1 Ballistic Coefficient = 0.250

Distance • Yards	Muzzle	100	200	300	400	500	600	800	1000
Velocity • fps	3680	3245	2852	2491	2158	1852	1577	1161	958
Energy • ft-lbs	1654	1287	994	758	569	419	304	165	112
Taylor KO Index	6.5	5.7	5.0	4.4	3.8	3.3	2.8	2.0	1.7
Path • Inches	-1.5	+0.9	0.0	-5.2	-16.1	-34.4	-63.1	-167.9	-375.9
Wind Drift • Inches	0.0	0.9	4.0	9.4	17.8	29.9	46.5	96.6	169.2

Federal 55-grain Sierra BlitzKing (P22250C)

G1 Ballistic Coefficient = 0.271

Distance • Yards	Muzzle	100	200	300	400	500	600	800	1000
Velocity • fps	3625	3230	2860	2530	2210	1930	1667	1244	1008
Energy • ft-lbs	1605	1270	1000	780	600	450	340	189	124
Taylor KO Index	6.4	5.7	5.0	4.5	3.9	3.4	2.9	2.2	1.8
Path • Inches	-1.5	+0.9	0.0	-5.2	-15.9	-33.7	-60.8	-157.3	-344.3
Wind Drift • Inches	0.0	0.9	3.7	8.7	16.4	27.4	42.3	86.9	153.2

Hornady 60-grain SP (8039)

G1 Ballistic Coefficient = 0.264

Distance • Yards	Muzzle	100	200	300	400	500	600	800	1000
Velocity • fps	3530	3131	2767	2431	2119	1832	1573	1175	972
Energy • ft-lbs	1660	1306	1020	787	598	447	330	184	126
Taylor KO Index	6.8	6.0	5.3	4.7	4.1	3.5	3.0	2.3	1.9
Path • Inches	-1.5	+1.0	0.0	-5.6	-17.1	-36.4	-66.2	-173.2	-381.0
Wind Drift • Inches	0.0	0.9	3.9	9.3	17.6	29.5	45.6	94.1	164.1

.243 Winchester

Black Hills 58-grain Hornady V-MAX (1C243BHGN6)

G1 Ballistic Coefficient = 0.250

Distance • Yards	Muzzle	100	200	300	400	500	600	800	1000
Velocity • fps	3800	3353	2950	2581	2241	1928	1644	1202	977
Energy • ft-lbs	1859	1448	1121	858	647	479	348	186	123
Taylor KO Index	7.7	6.8	5.9	5.2	4.5	3.9	3.3	2.4	2.0
Path • Inches	-1.5	+0.8	0.0	-4.8	-14.9	-32.0	-58.4	-155.3	-348.8
Wind Drift • Inches	0.0	0.9	3.8	9.0	17.1	28.6	44.4	92.3	163.9

Cor-Bon 70-grain BlitzKing (SD24370/20)

G1 Ballistic Coefficient = 0.290

Distance • Yards	Muzzle	100	200	300	400	500	600	800	1000
Velocity • fps	3700	3321	2974	2652	2353	2073	1814	1373	1084
Energy • ft-lbs	2128	1715	1375	1094	861	668	512	293	183
Taylor KO Index	9.0	7.8	7.0	6.2	5.5	4.8	4.2	3.2	2.6
Path • Inches	-1.5	+1.2	0.0	-6.1	-18.3	-38.5	-68.9	-174.6	-372.6
Wind Drift • Inches	0.0	0.9	3.7	8.8	16.6	27.6	42.5	86.4	150.3

Hornady 75-grain HP (8040)

G1 Ballistic Coefficient = 0.294

Distance • Yards	Muzzle	100	200	300	400	500	600	800	1000
Velocity • fps	3340	2996	2677	2380	2102	1844	1609	1230	1014
Energy • ft-lbs	1857	1494	1193	943	736	566	431	252	171
Taylor KO Index	8.7	7.8	7.0	6.2	5.5	4.8	4.2	3.2	2.6
Path • Inches	-1.5	+1.2	0.0	-6.1	-18.3	-38.5	-68.9	-174.6	-372.6
Wind Drift • Inches	0.0	0.9	3.7	8.8	16.6	27.6	42.5	86.4	150.3

Hornady 80-grain GMX (80456) ☺

G1 Ballistic Coefficient = 0.300

Distance • Yards	Muzzle	100	200	300	400	500	600	800	1000
Velocity • fps	3425	3080	2760	2463	2184	1924	1690	1293	1049
Energy • ft-lbs	2083	1684	1358	1077	847	657	507	297	195
Taylor KO Index	9.5	8.6	7.7	6.8	6.1	5.3	4.7	3.6	2.9
Path • Inches	-1.5	+1.1	0.0	-5.7	-17.1	-35.9	-63.9	-160.7	-341.6
Wind Drift • Inches	0.0	0.8	3.5	8.4	15.7	26.0	39.8	80.7	141.5

Remington 80-grain Copper Solid Tipped (PCS243WB) ☺

G1 Ballistic Coefficient = 0.299

Distance • Yards	Muzzle	100	200	300	400	500	600	800	1000
Velocity • fps	3350	3011	2696	2403	2128	1872	1638	1255	1029
Energy • ft-lbs	1993	1610	1291	1025	804	622	477	280	188
Taylor KO Index	9.3	8.1	7.2	6.4	5.7	5.0	4.4	3.3	2.6
Path • Inches	-1.5	+0.8	0.0	-4.8	-14.5	-30.6	-54.8	-138.5	-297.5
Wind Drift • Inches	0.0	0.8	3.3	7.9	14.7	24.4	37.3	75.9	134.8

Nosler 85-grain Partition (60002)

G1 Ballistic Coefficient = 0.315

Distance • Yards	Muzzle	100	200	300	400	500	600	800	1000
Velocity • fps	3225	2911	2618	2343	2086	1847	1626	1263	1041
Energy • ft-lbs	1963	1599	1294	1036	821	643	499	301	205
Taylor KO Index	9.5	8.6	7.7	6.9	6.2	5.4	4.8	3.7	3.1
Path • Inches	-1.5	+1.3	0.0	-6.4	-19.2	-39.9	-71.0	-176.6	-370.1
Wind Drift • Inches	0.0	0.9	3.6	8.6	16.1	26.6	40.7	82.0	142.3

Black Hills 85-grain Barnes TSX (1C243BHGN4) ☺

G1 Ballistic Coefficient = 0.333

Distance • Yards	Muzzle	100	200	300	400	500	600	800	1000
Velocity • fps	3200	2904	2628	2367	2122	1891	1678	1318	1080
Energy • ft-lbs	1932	1592	1303	1058	850	675	532	328	220
Taylor KO Index	9.4	8.6	7.8	7.0	6.3	5.6	5.0	3.9	3.2
Path • Inches	-1.5	+1.3	0.0	-6.4	-19.0	-39.3	-69.5	-170.4	-352.1
Wind Drift • Inches	0.0	0.8	3.4	8.1	15.2	25.0	38.2	76.4	132.7

Nosler 90-grain CT (10123)

G1 Ballistic Coefficient = 0.410

Distance • Yards	Muzzle	100	200	300	400	500	600	800	1000
Velocity • fps	3200	2958	2729	2511	2304	2107	1920	1580	1300
Energy • ft-lbs	2046	1748	1488	1260	1061	887	737	499	338
Taylor KO Index	10.0	9.2	8.5	7.8	7.2	6.6	6.0	4.9	4.1
Path • Inches	-1.5	+1.2	0.0	-5.9	-17.4	-35.4	-61.2	-143.3	-281.9
Wind Drift • Inches	0.0	0.7	2.8	6.4	11.9	19.3	29.1	56.8	97.7

Hornady 95-grain SST (80463)

G1 Ballistic Coefficient = 0.355

Distance • Yards	Muzzle	100	200	300	400	500	600	800	1000
Velocity • fps	3185	2908	2648	2402	2169	1950	1690	1293	1048
Energy • ft-lbs	2139	1784	1478	1217	992	802	643	407	271
Taylor KO Index	10.5	9.6	8.4	7.9	7.2	6.4	5.8	4.6	3.7
Path • Inches	-1.5	+1.3	0.0	-6.3	-18.6	-38.4	-67.3	-162.5	-330.6
Wind Drift • Inches	0.0	0.8	3.2	7.6	14.1	23.2	35.3	70.1	121.7

Winchester 100-grain Power Max Bonded (X243BP)

G1 Ballistic Coefficient = 0.372

Distance • Yards	Muzzle	100	200	300	400	500	600	800	1000
Velocity • fps	2960	2708	2470	2240	2031	1829	1642	1323	1101
Energy • ft-lbs	1945	1628	1355	1118	915	743	599	389	269
Taylor KO Index	10.3	9.4	8.6	7.8	7.1	6.3	5.7	4.6	3.8
Path • Inches	-1.5	+1.6	0.0	-7.3	-21.6	-44.3	-77.5	-185.8	-374.2
Wind Drift • Inches	0.0	0.8	3.4	8.0	14.9	24.4	37.1	73.2	125.6

Cor-Bon 115-grain DTAC (PM243115/20)

G1 Ballistic Coefficient = 0.360

Distance • Yards	Muzzle	100	200	300	400	500	600	800	1000
Velocity • fps	2900	2644	2401	2172	1955	1753	1567	1257	1058
Energy • ft-lbs	2148	1785	1473	1205	977	785	627	404	286
Taylor KO Index	11.6	10.6	9.6	8.7	7.8	7.0	6.3	5.0	4.2
Path • Inches	-1.5	+1.7	0.0	-7.8	-23.0	-47.3	-83.0	-200.6	-406.7
Wind Drift • Inches	0.0	0.9	3.6	8.5	16.0	23.0	39.9	79.1	134.9

6mm Remington

Hornady 95-grain SST (81663)

G1 Ballistic Coefficient = 0.355

Distance • Yards	Muzzle	100	200	300	400	500	600	800	1000
Velocity • fps	3235	2955	2692	2443	2209	1987	1779	1417	1151
Energy • ft-lbs	2207	1841	1528	1259	1029	833	668	484	279
Taylor KO Index	10.7	9.7	8.9	8.1	7.3	6.6	5.9	4.7	3.8
Path • Inches	-1.5	+1.6	0.0	-6.1	-18.0	-37.0	-64.9	-156.6	-318.5
Wind Drift • Inches	0.0	0.8	3.2	7.4	13.8	22.7	34.5	68.5	119.0

.243 Winchester Super Short Magnum (WSSM)

Winchester 95-grain Ballistic Silvertip (SBST243SSA)

G1 Ballistic Coefficient = 0.410

Distance • Yards	Muzzle	100	200	300	400	500	600	800	1000
Velocity • fps	3150	2905	2674	2453	2244	2045	1859	1521	1250
Energy • ft-lbs	2093	1780	1508	1270	1062	882	729	488	330
Taylor KO Index	10.4	9.6	8.8	8.1	7.4	6.7	6.1	5.0	4.1
Path • Inches	-1.5	+1.3	0.0	-6.2	-18.2	-37.1	-64.2	-151.1	-298.9
Wind Drift • Inches	0.0	0.7	2.9	6.7	12.4	20.3	30.6	60.0	103.3

.257 Roberts

Hornady 117-grain SST + P (81353)

G1 Ballistic Coefficient = 0.390

Distance • Yards	Muzzle	100	200	300	400	500	600	800	1000
Velocity • fps	2946	2705	2478	2265	2057	1863	1683	1368	1137
Energy • ft-lbs	2253	1901	1595	1329	1099	902	736	486	336
Taylor KO Index	12.0	11.0	10.1	9.2	8.4	7.6	6.8	5.6	4.6
Path • Inches	-1.5	+1.6	0.0	-7.3	-21.4	-43.8	-76.1	-80.7	-360.4
Wind Drift • Inches	0.0	0.8	3.2	7.6	14.2	23.2	35.1	69.0	118.3

Federal 12010-grain Nosler Partition + P (P257B)

G1 Ballistic Coefficient = 0.393

This load is now identified as +P

.25-06 Remington

Federal 85-grain Nosler Ballistic Tip (P2506G)

G1 Ballistic Coefficient = 0.329

Distance • Yards	Muzzle	100	200	300	400	500	600	800	1000
Velocity • fps	3550	3230	2930	2640	2380	2130	1896	1485	1178
Energy • ft-lbs	2380	1965	1615	1320	1070	855	679	416	262
Taylor KO Index	11.1	10.1	9.1	8.2	7.4	6.6	5.9	4.6	3.7
Path • Inches	-1.5	+0.9	0.0	-5.0	-15.0	-31.2	-55.0	-134.6	-278.5
Wind Drift • Inches	0.0	0.7	3.0	7.2	13.4	21.9	33.3	66.6	117.2

Federal 100-grain Barnes Triple-Shock X-Bullet (P2506H) ☺

G1 Ballistic Coefficient = 0.421

Distance • Yards	Muzzle	100	200	300	400	500	600	800	1000
Velocity • fps	3210	2970	2750	2540	2330	2140	1956	1619	1337
Energy • ft-lbs	2290	1965	1680	1430	1205	1015	850	582	397
Taylor KO Index	11.8	10.9	10.1	9.3	8.6	7.9	7.2	5.9	4.9
Path • Inches	-1.5	+1.2	0.0	-5.8	-17.0	-34.8	-59.9	-139.6	-273.1
Wind Drift • Inches	0.0	0.6	2.7	6.2	11.4	18.6	28.0	54.5	93.5

Black Hills 117-grain Hornady SST (1C2506BHGN3)

G1 Ballistic Coefficient = 0.390

Distance • Yards	Muzzle	100	200	300	400	500	600	800	1000
Velocity • fps	3150	2899	2662	2437	2223	2020	1828	1486	1218
Energy • ft-lbs	2577	2184	1841	1543	1284	1060	869	574	386
Taylor KO Index	13.5	12.5	11.4	10.5	9.5	8.7	7.9	6.4	5.2
Path • Inches	-1.5	+1.3	0.0	-6.2	-18.4	-37.5	-65.2	-154.4	-307.2
Wind Drift • Inches	0.0	0.7	3.0	6.9	12.8	21.0	31.7	62.4	107.6

Hornady 117-grain SST (81453)

G1 Ballistic Coefficient = 0.390

Distance • Yards	Muzzle	100	200	300	400	500	600	800	1000
Velocity • fps	3110	2861	2626	2403	2191	1989	1800	1463	1207
Energy • ft-lbs	2512	2127	1792	1500	1246	1028	842	556	375
Taylor KO Index	13.4	12.1	11.3	10.3	9.4	8.5	7.7	6.3	5.2
Path • Inches	-1.5	+1.6	0.0	-6.4	-18.9	-38.6	-67.2	-159.1	-316.8
Wind Drift • Inches	0.0	0.7	3.0	7.0	13.1	21.4	32.3	63.9	109.6

.257 Weatherby Magnum

Weatherby 80-grain Barnes TTSX (B25780TTSX) ☺

G1 Ballistic Coefficient = 0.378

Distance • Yards	Muzzle	100	200	300	400	500	600	800	1000
Velocity • fps	3870	3561	3274	3005	2753	2514	2290	1873	1511
Energy • ft-lbs	2661	2254	1906	1606	1348	1125	931	623	406
Taylor KO Index	11.4	10.5	9.6	8.8	8.1	7.4	6.7	5.5	4.4
Path • Inches	-1.5	+0.6	0.0	-3.9	-11.6	-23.9	-41.7	-98.8.	-196.2
Wind Drift • Inches	0.0	0.6	2.4	5.6	10.5	16.7	25.1	48.8	84.4

Weatherby 100-grain Spitzer (G257100SR)

G1 Ballistic Coefficient = 0.256

Distance • Yards	Muzzle	100	200	300	400	500	600	800	1000
Velocity • fps	3500	3091	2718	2375	2057	1766	1505	1126	944
Energy • ft-lbs	2721	2122	1641	1253	940	693	5.3	282	198
Taylor KO Index	12.9	11.3	10.0	8.7	7.6	6.5	5.5	4.1	3.5
Path • Inches	-1.5	+1.1	0.0	-5.8	-17.8	-38.2	-69.8	-184.9	-409.2
Wind Drift • Inches	0.0	1.0	4.1	9.8	18.6	31.3	48.6	100.4	173.7

Weatherby 117-grain Barnes TSX (B257100TSX) ☺

G1 Ballistic Coefficient = 0.420

Distance • Yards	Muzzle	100	200	300	400	500	600	800	1000
Velocity • fps	3570	3312	3079	2840	2623	2416	2218	1850	1527
Energy • ft-lbs	2831	2437	2094	1793	1528	1296	1092	760	518
Taylor KO Index	13.1	12.2	11.3	10.4	9.6	8.9	8.1	6.8	5.6
Path • Inches	-1.5	+0.8	0.0	-4.5	-13.4	-27.3	-47.2	-109.6	-213.1
Wind Drift • Inches	0.0	0.6	2.3	5.4	10.0	16.2	24.2	46.8	80.1

6.5x57 Mauser

Sellier & Bellot 131-grain SP (V330622U)

G1 Ballistic Coefficient = 0.343

Distance • Yards	Muzzle	100	200	300	400	500	600	800	1000
Velocity • fps	2543	2295	2060	1841	1638	1455	1296	1073	949
Energy • ft-lbs	1882	1532	1235	986	780	616	489	335	262
Taylor KO Index	12.6	11.3	10.2	9.1	8.1	7.2	6.4	5.3	4.7
Path • Inches	-1.5	+2.6	0.0	-10.8	-31.9	-66.0	-116.6	-284.8	-573.4
Wind Drift • Inches	0.0	1.1	4.6	11.0	20.6	34.1	51.8	100.6	164.3

6.5x55 Swedish Mauser

Lapua 100-grain FMJ (4316033)

G1 Ballistic Coefficient = 0.250

Distance • Yards	Muzzle	100	200	300	400	500	600	800	1000
Velocity • fps	2725	2374	2049	1752	1491	1273	1113	935	829
Energy • ft-lbs	1649	1251	932	682	494	360	275	194	152
Taylor KO Index	10.3	9.0	7.7	6.6	5.6	4.8	4.8	3.5	3.1
Path • Inches	-1.5	+2.4	0.0	-10.7	-32.8	-70.7	-130.1	-339.0	-706.8
Wind Drift • Inches	0.0	1.4	6.0	14.4	27.7	46.8	71.9	137.6	219.3

Lapua 108-grain Scenar HPBT (C316031)

G1 Ballistic Coefficient = 0.458

Distance • Yards	Muzzle	100	200	300	400	500	600	800	1000
Velocity • fps	3015	2811	2612	2418	2236	2062	1896	1592	1280
Energy • ft-lbs	2180	1895	1636	1402	1199	1020	862	608	393
Taylor KO Index	12.3	11.4	10.6	9.8	9.1	8.4	7.7	6.5	5.2
Path • Inches	-1.5	+1.5	0.0	-6.6	-19.1	-38.6	-66.3	-152.6	-294.4
Wind Drift • Inches	0.0	0.6	2.6	6.2	11.4	18.4	27.6	53.4	91.0

Lapua 108-grain Scenar HPBT (4316031)

G1 Ballistic Coefficient = 0.453

Distance • Yards	Muzzle	100	200	300	400	500	600	800	1000
Velocity • fps	2953	2748	2550	2358	2177	2003	1838	1539	1238
Energy • ft-lbs	2087	1811	1590	1333	1136	962	811	568	400
Taylor KO Index	12.0	11.2	10.4	9.6	8.9	8.2	7.5	6.3	5.0
Path • Inches	-1.5	+1.6	0.0	-6.9	-20.1	-40.7	-69.9	-161.3	-312.0
Wind Drift • Inches	0.0	0.7	2.8	6.4	11.8	19.2	28.9	56.0	95.3

Lapua 123-grain Scenar HPBT (4316036)

G1 Ballistic Coefficient = 0.525

Distance • Yards	Muzzle	100	200	300	400	500	600	800	1000
Velocity • fps	3015	2836	2661	2490	2328	2172	2022	1742	1457
Energy • ft-lbs	2492	2204	1941	1699	1481	1298	1117	829	582
Taylor KO Index	14.0	13.2	12.3	11.6	10.8	10.1	9.4	8.1	6.8
Path • Inches	-1.5	+1.4	0.0	-6.3	-18.3	-36.7	-62.4	-140.9	-265.5
Wind Drift • Inches	0.0	0.6	2.3	5.3	9.7	15.7	23.4	44.6	75.1

Lapua 123-grain Scenar HPBT (C316032)

G1 Ballistic Coefficient = 0.520

Distance • Yards	Muzzle	100	200	300	400	500	600	800	1000
Velocity • fps	2930	2743	2571	2401	2241	2087	1939	1664	1391
Energy • ft-lbs	2337	2063	1811	1580	1372	1190	1027	757	550
Taylor KO Index	13.5	12.7	11.9	11.1	10.4	9.7	9.0	7.7	6.5
Path • Inches	-1.5	+1.6	0.0	-6.8	-19.7	-39.6	-67.4	-152.3	-287.9
Wind Drift • Inches	0.0	0.6	2.4	5.6	10.3	16.6	24.8	47.4	79.9

Lapua 123-grain Scenar HPBT (4316032)

G1 Ballistic Coefficient = 0.514

Distance • Yards	Muzzle	100	200	300	400	500	600	800	1000
Velocity • fps	2720	2548	2379	2217	2062	1914	1773	1515	1253
Energy • ft-lbs	2028	1779	1551	1347	1162	1001	859	627	430
Taylor KO Index	12.6	11.8	11.0	10.3	9.6	8.9	8.2	7.0	5.8
Path • Inches	-1.5	+1.9	0.0	-8.1	-23.3	-46.6	-79.5	-180.3	-342.3
Wind Drift • Inches	0.0	0.6	2.7	6.3	11.6	18.7	28.0	53.6	90.3

Lapua 123-grain Scenar HPBT (C316032)

G1 Ballistic Coefficient = 0.514

Distance • Yards	Muzzle	100	200	300	400	500	600	800	1000
Velocity • fps	2720	2548	2379	2217	2062	1914	1773	1515	1253
Energy • ft-lbs	2028	1779	1551	1347	1162	1001	859	627	430
Taylor KO Index	12.6	11.8	11.0	10.3	9.6	8.9	8.2	7.0	5.8
Path • Inches	-1.5	+1.9	0.0	-8.1	-23.3	-46.6	-79.5	-180.3	-342.3
Wind Drift • Inches	0.0	0.6	2.7	6.3	11.6	18.7	28.0	53.6	90.3

Lapua 139-grain Scenar HPBT (C316030)

G1 Ballistic Coefficient = 0.575

Distance • Yards	Muzzle	100	200	300	400	500	600	800	1000
Velocity • fps	2740	2568	2435	2289	2145	2009	1878	1634	1402
Energy • ft-lbs	2315	2062	1828	1615	1420	1246	1089	825	606
Taylor KO Index	14.4	13.6	12.8	12.0	11.2	10.5	9.8	8.6	7.3
Path • Inches	-1.5	+1.9	0.0	-7.7	-22.1	-44.1	-74.7	-167.0	-311.6
Wind Drift • Inches	0.0	0.6	2.4	5.5	10.1	16.2	24.2	45.9	76.9

Lapua 139-grain Scenar HPBT (4316030)

G1 Ballistic Coefficient = 0.575

Distance • Yards	Muzzle	100	200	300	400	500	600	800	1000
Velocity • fps	2620	2468	2320	2178	2040	1908	1782	1548	1317
Energy • ft-lbs	2117	1878	1660	1463	1285	1124	980	740	535
Taylor KO Index	13.7	12.9	12.2	11.4	10.7	10.0	9.3	8.1	6.9
Path • Inches	-1.5	+2.1	0.0	-8.6	-24.5	-48.8	-82.6	-184.8	-345.4
Wind Drift • Inches	0.0	0.6	2.5	5.9	10.8	18.0	25.8	49.2	82.1

Lapua 155-grain Mega (4316021)

G1 Ballistic Coefficient = 0.377

Distance • Yards	Muzzle	100	200	300	400	500	600	800	1000
Velocity • fps	2560	2332	2116	1912	1712	1547	1399	1145	1001
Energy • ft-lbs	2254	1871	1540	1257	1021	823	664	451	345
Taylor KO Index	15.0	13.6	12.4	11.2	10.0	9.0	8.2	6.7	5.9
Path • Inches	-1.5	+2.4	0.0	-10.2	-30.0	-61.6	-107.9	-258.2	-514.6
Wind Drift • Inches	0.0	1.0	4.1	9.7	18.2	30.0	45.4	88.3	146.3

.260 Remington

Federal 120-grain Barnes Triple-Shock X-Bullet (P260C) ☺

G1 Ballistic Coefficient = 0.381

Distance • Yards	Muzzle	100	200	300	400	500	600	800	1000
Velocity • fps	2930	2690	2450	2240	2030	1830	1647	1333	1112
Energy • ft-lbs	2285	1920	1605	1330	1095	890	723	474	329
Taylor KO Index	13.3	12.2	11.1	10.1	9.2	8.3	7.5	6.0	5.0
Path • Inches	-1.5	+1.7	0.0	-7.6	-21.9	-44.7	-78.2	-186.6	-373.8
Wind Drift • Inches	0.0	0.8	3.4	7.9	14.7	24.1	36.5	71.9	123.2

Cor-Bon 123-grain Scenar (PM260123/20)

G1 Ballistic Coefficient = 0.520

Distance • Yards	Muzzle	100	200	300	400	500	600	800	1000
Velocity • fps	2950	2769	2595	2428	2267	2111	1963	1686	1442
Energy • ft-lbs	2377	2095	1840	1610	1403	1218	1052	776	568
Taylor KO Index	13.7	12.8	12.0	11.3	10.5	9.8	9.1	7.8	6.7
Path • Inches	-1.5	+1.5	0.0	-6.7	-19.3	-38.7	-65.8	-148.8	-281.1
Wind Drift • Inches	0.0	0.6	2.4	5.5	10.1	16.4	24.4	46.7	78.7

Cor-Bon 139-grain Scenar (PM260139/20)

G1 Ballistic Coefficient = 0.575

Distance • Yards	Muzzle	100	200	300	400	500	600	800	1000
Velocity • fps	2750	2593	2442	2295	2154	2017	1886	1641	1425
Energy • ft-lbs	2335	2076	1840	1626	1432	1256	1098	832	627
Taylor KO Index	14.4	13.6	12.8	12.0	11.3	10.6	9.9	8.6	7.5
Path • Inches	-1.5	+1.8	0.0	-7.7	-22.0	-43.8	-74.1	-165.6	-309.0
Wind Drift • Inches	0.0	0.6	2.4	5.5	10.0	16.2	24.0	45.7	76.4

Nosler 140-grain Partition (13063)

G1 Ballistic Coefficient = 0.486

Distance • Yards	Muzzle	100	200	300	400	500	600	800	1000
Velocity • fps	2725	2542	2367	2198	2037	1884	1737	1472	1254
Energy • ft-lbs	2308	2009	1741	1502	1290	1103	938	673	489
Taylor KO Index	14.4	13.4	12.5	11.6	10.8	9.9	9.2	7.8	6.6
Path • Inches	-1.5	+1.9	0.0	-8.1	-23.5	-47.2	-80.7	-184.5	-353.0
Wind Drift • Inches	0.0	0.7	2.8	6.6	12.2	19.8	29.6	57.0	96.3

Cor-Bon 142-grain HPBT (PM260142/20)

G1 Ballistic Coefficient = 0.480

Distance • Yards	Muzzle	100	200	300	400	500	600	800	1000
Velocity • fps	2700	2515	2337	2166	2003	1847	1700	1436	1223
Energy • ft-lbs	2299	1994	1722	1480	1265	1076	911	650	472
Taylor KO Index	14.5	13.5	12.5	11.6	10.7	9.9	9.1	7.7	6.5
Path • Inches	-1.5	+2.0	0.0	-8.4	-24.2	-48.7	-83.4	-191.2	-367.0
Wind Drift • Inches	0.0	0.7	2.9	6.8	12.6	20.5	30.8	59.4	100.2

6.5 Creedmore

This cartridge is another variant of a 6.5 / .308. It has attained some popularity among long-range shooters in practical style events. In 2008, Hornady announced that it would be building ammo for this cartridge. Performance-wise, it is difficult to tell this cartridge from the .260 Remington, but competition shooting is as much of a mind game as it is a shooting skill, so you shoot what you think works best. With proper bullets, this cartridge is entirely suitable for light game.

Hornady 120-grain A-MAX (81492)

G1 Ballistic Coefficient = 0.480

Distance • Yards	Muzzle	100	200	300	400	500	600	800	1000
Velocity • fps	2910	2712	2522	2340	2166	1999	1839	1549	1306
Energy • ft-lbs	2256	1959	1695	1459	1250	1065	901	639	454
Taylor KO Index	13.2	12.3	11.4	10.6	9.8	9.0	8.3	7.0	5.9
Path • Inches	-1.5	+1.6	0.0	-7.1	-20.5	-41.4	-71.1	-163.2	-313.8
Wind Drift • Inches	0.0	0.6	2.7	6.3	11.6	18.9	28.3	54.6	92.8

Hornady 129-grain SST (81496)

G1 Ballistic Coefficient = 0.480

Distance • Yards	Muzzle	100	200	300	400	500	600	800	1000
Velocity • fps	2950	2756	2570	2392	2221	2057	1900	1612	1364
Energy • ft-lbs	2492	2175	1892	1639	1417	1212	1035	744	533
Taylor KO Index	14.4	13.4	12.5	11.6	10.8	10.0	9.2	7.8	6.6
Path • Inches	-1.5	+1.5	0.0	-6.8	-19.7	-39.5	-67.8	-154.9	-296.0
Wind Drift • Inches	0.0	0.6	2.6	6.0	11.0	17.8	26.6	51.2	86.7

Hornady 140-grain A-MAX (81494)

G1 Ballistic Coefficient = 0.480

Distance • Yards	Muzzle	100	200	300	400	500	600	800	1000
Velocity • fps	2710	2557	2409	2266	2128	1995	1867	1628	1417
Energy • ft-lbs	2283	2032	1804	1596	1408	1235	1084	824	625
Taylor KO Index	14.3	13.5	12.7	12.0	11.2	10.5	9.9	8.6	7.5
Path • Inches	-1.5	+1.9	0.0	-7.9	-22.6	-45.0	-76.1	-169.7	-316.2
Wind Drift • Inches	0.0	0.6	2.4	5.5	10.0	16.2	24.1	45.7	76.3

6.8 Remington SPC

Hornady 100-grain V-MAX (8346)

G1 Ballistic Coefficient = 0.370

Distance • Yards	Muzzle	100	200	300	400	500	600	800	1000
Velocity • fps	2570	2338	2118	1910	1716	1538	1379	1135	993
Energy • ft-lbs	1613	1335	1095	891	719	577	465	315	241
Taylor KO Index	11.1	10.1	9.1	8.2	7.4	6.6	5.9	4.9	4.3
Path • Inches	-1.5	+2.4	0.0	-10.2	-30.0	-61.6	-108.0	-260.0	-519.7
Wind Drift • Inches	0.0	1.0	4.2	9.9	18.5	30.5	46.2	90.1	149.0

Hornady 110-grain BTHP (8146)

G1 Ballistic Coefficient = 0.360

Distance • Yards	Muzzle	100	200	300	400	500	600	800	1000
Velocity • fps	2570	2332	2106	1893	1695	1514	1355	1115	979
Energy • ft-lbs	1613	1328	1083	875	702	560	448	304	234
Taylor KO Index	11.1	10.0	9.1	8.2	7.3	6.5	5.8	4.8	4.2
Path • Inches	-1.5	+2.5	0.0	-10.3	-30.4	-62.6	-110.0	-266.2	-534.1
Wind Drift • Inches	0.0	1.0	4.3	10.2	19.1	31.6	47.9	93.3	154.0

Cor-Bon 110-grain DPX (DPX68110/20) ☺

G1 Ballistic Coefficient = 0.350

Distance • Yards	Muzzle	100	200	300	400	500	600	800	1000
Velocity • fps	2400	2164	1942	1735	1548	1377	1235	1042	932
Energy • ft-lbs	1407	1144	922	735	584	463	372	265	212
Taylor KO Index	10.3	9.3	8.4	7.5	6.7	5.9	5.3	4.5	4.0
Path • Inches	-1.5	+3.0	0.0	-12.2	-36.1	-74.5	-131.4	-318.2	-632.9
Wind Drift • Inches	0.0	1.2	4.9	11.7	22.0	36.2	54.7	104.6	168.3

.270 Winchester

Winchester 130-grain Power Max Bonded (S2705BP)

G1 Ballistic Coefficient = 0.341

Distance • Yards	Muzzle	100	200	300	400	500	600	800	1000
Velocity • fps	3060	2779	2515	2266	2032	1814	1613	1277	1061
Energy • ft-lbs	2702	2229	1826	1482	1191	950	752	471	325
Taylor KO Index	15.6	14.1	12.8	11.5	10.3	9.2	8.2	6.5	5.4
Path • Inches	-1.5	+1.5	0.0	-7.0	-20.8	-42.6	-75.9	-185.4	-380.9
Wind Drift • Inches	0.0	0.8	3.6	8.4	15.7	26.0	39.6	78.9	135.9

Federal 130-grain Trophy Bonded Tip (P270TT4)

G1 Ballistic Coefficient = 0.439

Distance • Yards	Muzzle	100	200	300	400	500	600	800	1000
Velocity • fps	3200	2970	2760	2560	2360	2170	1933	1664	1384
Energy • ft-lbs	2955	2555	2200	1885	1610	1365	1147	800	553
Taylor KO Index	16.3	15.1	14.0	13.0	12.0	11.0	10.1	8.5	7.0
Path • Inches	-1.5	+1.2	0.0	-5.8	-16.9	-34.3	-59.1	-136.7	-265.1
Wind Drift • Inches	0.0	0.6	2.6	5.9	11.0	17.8	26.7	51.7	88.4

Hornady 130-grain SST (80543)

G1 Ballistic Coefficient = 0.460

Distance • Yards	Muzzle	100	200	300	400	500	600	800	1000
Velocity • fps	3200	2984	2788	2582	2393	2213	2041	1721	1443
Energy • ft-lbs	2955	2570	2228	1924	1653	1414	1203	855	601
Taylor KO Index	16.3	15.2	14.2	13.1	12.2	11.3	10.4	8.8	7.3
Path • Inches	-1.5	+1.2	0.0	-5.7	-16.7	-33.7	-57.8	-132.7	-255.0
Wind Drift • Inches	0.0	0.6	2.4	5.6	10.4	16.8	25.2	48.5	82.6

Hornady 130-grain GMX (8052) ☺

G1 Ballistic Coefficient = 0.459

Distance • Yards	Muzzle	100	200	300	400	500	600	800	1000
Velocity • fps	3190	2976	2769	2573	2385	2202	2031	1712	1435
Energy • ft-lbs	2937	2553	2213	1911	1642	1404	1191	846	594
Taylor KO Index	16.2	15.1	14.1	13.1	12.1	11.2	10.3	8.7	7.3
Path • Inches	-1.5	+1.2	0.0	-5.5	-16.8	-33.9	-58.3	-133.8	-257.4
Wind Drift • Inches	0.0	0.6	2.4	5.7	10.5	16.9	25.4	48.9	83.3

Hornady 130-grain SST (8054)

G1 Ballistic Coefficient = 0.460

Distance • Yards	Muzzle	100	200	300	400	500	600	800	1000
Velocity • fps	3060	2851	2651	2460	2277	2101	1934	1627	1365
Energy • ft-lbs	2702	2345	2028	1746	1496	1275	1080	764	538
Taylor KO Index	15.6	14.5	13.5	12.5	11.6	10.7	9.8	8.3	6.9
Path • Inches	-1.5	+1.4	0.0	-6.3	-18.5	-37.3	-64.0	-147.1	-283.3
Wind Drift • Inches	0.0	0.6	2.6	6.0	11.0	17.9	26.9	51.9	88.4

Remington 130-grain Copper Solid Tipped (PCS270WA) ☺

G1 Ballistic Coefficient = 0.431

Distance • Yards	Muzzle	100	200	300	400	500	600	800	1000
Velocity • fps	3060	2837	2625	2422	2229	2044	1869	1551	1289
Energy • ft-lbs	2702	2323	1988	1693	1434	1206	1009	695	480
Taylor KO Index	15.6	14.4	13.4	12.3	11.3	10.4	9.5	7.9	6.6
Path • Inches	-1.5	+1.4	0.0	-6.5	-18.9	-38.3	-66.1	-153.5	-299.5
Wind Drift • Inches	0.0	0.7	2.8	6.4	11.9	19.4	29.2	56.7	97.1

Winchester 130-grain E-Tip (S270WET) ☺

G1 Ballistic Coefficient = 0.459

Distance • Yards	Muzzle	100	200	300	400	500	600	800	1000
Velocity • fps	3050	2841	2641	2450	2267	2092	1925	1618	1357
Energy • ft-lbs	2685	2329	2013	1732	1483	1263	1069	756	531
Taylor KO Index	15.5	14.5	13.4	12.5	11.5	10.6	9.8	8.2	6.9
Path • Inches	-1.5	+1.4	0.0	-6.4	-18.6	-37.6	-64.5	-148.4	-286.0
Wind Drift • Inches	0.0	0.6	2.6	6.0	11.1	18.1	27.1	52.3	89.1

Hornady 140-grain SST (80563)

G1 Ballistic Coefficient = 0.495

Distance • Yards	Muzzle	100	200	300	400	500	600	800	1000
Velocity • fps	3090	2894	2706	2526	2353	2187	2028	1731	1469
Energy • ft-lbs	2968	2603	2276	1988	1721	1487	1278	931	671
Taylor KO Index	16.9	15.9	14.8	13.8	12.9	12.0	11.1	9.5	8.1
Path • Inches	-1.5	+1.3	0.0	-6.1	-17.6	-35.4	-60.6	-137.6	-261.5
Wind Drift • Inches	0.0	0.6	2.4	5.5	10.0	16.2	24.2	46.4	75.5

Federal 140-grain Nosler AccuBond (P270A1)

G1 Ballistic Coefficient = 0.499

Distance • Yards	Muzzle	100	200	300	400	500	600	800	1000
Velocity • fps	2950	2760	2580	2400	2240	2080	1926	1642	1396
Energy • ft-lbs	2705	2370	2065	1795	1555	1340	1154	838	606
Taylor KO Index	16.2	15.1	14.1	13.2	12.3	11.4	10.6	9.0	7.7
Path • Inches	-1.5	+1.5	0.0	-6.7	-19.5	-39.3	-67.0	-152.3	-289.6
Wind Drift • Inches	0.0	0.6	2.5	5.8	10.6	17.2	25.7	49.3	83.3

Federal 150-grain Trophy Bonded Tip (P270T2)

G1 Ballistic Coefficient = 0.473

Distance • Yards	Muzzle	100	200	300	400	500	600	800	1000
Velocity • fps	2830	2640	2450	2270	2100	1940	1785	1505	1273
Energy • ft-lbs	2665	2315	1995	1715	1465	1245	1062	754	540
Taylor KO Index	16.6	15.5	14.4	13.3	12.3	11.4	10.5	8.8	7.5
Path • Inches	-1.5	+1.7	0.0	-7.6	-22.0	-44.0	-75.4	-173.1	-332.7
Wind Drift • Inches	0.0	0.7	2.8	6.5	12.0	19.5	29.2	56.4	95.5

.270 Winchester Short Magnum

Winchester 130-grain XP³ (SXP270SA)

G1 Ballistic Coefficient = 0.436

Distance • Yards	Muzzle	100	200	300	400	500	600	800	1000
Velocity • fps	3275	3043	2824	2614	2415	2224	2042	1707	1417
Energy • ft-lbs	3096	2673	2301	1973	1683	1427	1205	841	580
Taylor KO Index	16.8	15.7	14.5	13.4	12.4	11.4	10.5	8.8	7.3
Path • Inches	-1.5	+1.1	0.0	-5.5	-16.1	-32.7	-56.2	-130.1	-252.4
Wind Drift • Inches	0.0	0.6	2.5	5.8	10.7	17.4	26.0	50.3	86.1

Federal 150-grain Trophy Bonded Tip (P270WSMTT2)

G1 Ballistic Coefficient = 0.469

Distance • Yards	Muzzle	100	200	300	400	500	600	800	1000
Velocity • fps	3100	2890	2700	2510	2330	2150	1984	1676	1410
Energy • ft-lbs	3200	2790	2420	2065	1800	1540	1311	936	662
Taylor KO Index	18.2	17.0	15.9	14.7	13.7	12.6	11.6	9.8	8.3
Path • Inches	-1.5	+1.3	0.0	-6.1	-17.7	-35.9	-61.6	-141.0	-270.5
Wind Drift • Inches	0.0	0.6	2.5	8.8	10.6	17.2	25.7	49.6	84.3

Nosler 150-grain Partition (15220)

G1 Ballistic Coefficient = 0.473

Distance • Yards	Muzzle	100	200	300	400	500	600	800	1000
Velocity • fps	3000	2798	2607	2422	2246	2077	1915	1618	1364
Energy • ft-lbs	2997	2607	2263	1954	1680	1437	1222	872	620
Taylor KO Index	17.6	16.4	15.3	14.2	13.2	12.2	11.2	9.5	8.0
Path • Inches	-1.5	+1.5	0.0	-6.6	-19.1	-38.6	-66.1	-151.8	-290.2
Wind Drift • Inches	0.0	0.6	2.6	6.0	11.0	17.9	26.7	51.6	87.6

.270 Weatherby

Weatherby 110-grain Barnes TTSX (B270110TTSX) ☺

G1 Ballistic Coefficient = 0.377

Distance • Yards	Muzzle	100	200	300	400	500	600	800	1000
Velocity • fps	3540	3253	2985	2733	2495	2269	2056	1667	1343
Energy • ft-lbs	3062	2586	2178	1825	1521	1258	1033	679	441
Taylor KO Index	15.2	14.0	12.9	11.8	10.7	9.8	8.9	7.2	5.8
Path • Inches	-1.5	+0.9	0.0	-4.8	-14.3	-29.3	-51.2	-121.4	-242.6
Wind Drift • Inches	0.0	0.6	2.7	6.2	11.5	18.8	28.3	55.6	96.5

Federal 130-grain Barnes Triple-Shock X-Bullet (P270WBC) ☺

G1 Ballistic Coefficient = 0.429

Distance • Yards	Muzzle	100	200	300	400	500	600	800	1000
Velocity • fps	3200	2970	2750	2540	2340	2150	1969	1639	1355
Energy • ft-lbs	2955	2545	2185	1865	1585	1340	1110	773	530
Taylor KO Index	16.3	15.1	14.0	12.9	11.9	10.9	10.0	8.3	6.9
Path • Inches	-1.5	+1.2	0.0	-6.8	-17.0	-34.6	-59.8	-138.8	-270.5
Wind Drift • Inches	0.0	0.6	2.6	6.1	11.2	18.3	27.5	53.3	91.4

Nosler 150-grain Partition (15085)

G1 Ballistic Coefficient = 0.495

Distance • Yards	Muzzle	100	200	300	400	500	600	800	1000
Velocity • fps	3150	2951	2761	2579	2404	2236	2074	1773	1505
Energy • ft-lbs	3305	2901	2539	2215	1925	1663	1433	1047	755
Taylor KO Index	18.5	17.3	16.2	15.1	14.1	13.1	12.2	10.4	8.8
Path • Inches	-1.5	+1.2	0.0	-5.8	-16.9	-33.9	-58.0	-131.7	-250.1
Wind Drift • Inches	0.0	0.6	2.3	5.3	9.8	15.8	23.5	45.1	76.3

7x57 Mauser

Sellier & Bellot 139-grain SP (V330902U)

G1 Ballistic Coefficient = 0.250

Distance • Yards	Muzzle	100	200	300	400	500	600	800	1000
Velocity • fps	2651	2306	1987	1697	1443	1235	1088	923	819
Energy • ft-lbs	2170	1641	1219	889	642	471	365	263	207
Taylor KO Index	15.0	13.0	11.2	9.6	8.1	7.0	6.1	5.2	4.6
Path • Inches	-1.5	+2.6	0.0	-11.4	-35.0	-75.5	-138.8	-359.2	-743.1
Wind Drift • Inches	0.0	1.4	6.2	15.0	28.9	48.6	74.5	140.9	223.0

Hornady 139-grain GMX (81556) ☺

G1 Ballistic Coefficient = 0.487

Distance • Yards	Muzzle	100	200	300	400	500	600	800	1000
Velocity • fps	2740	2555	2378	2208	2045	1889	1743	1475	1256
Energy • ft-lbs	2317	2015	1745	1504	1290	1101	938	672	487
Taylor KO Index	14.4	13.4	12.5	11.6	10.8	9.9	9.2	7.8	6.6
Path • Inches	-1.5	+1.9	0.0	-8.1	-23.3	-46.8	-80.1	-183.1	-350.6
Wind Drift • Inches	0.0	0.7	2.8	6.6	12.2	19.7	29.6	57.0	96.2

Hornady 139-grain SST (81553)

G1 Ballistic Coefficient = 0.486

Distance • Yards	Muzzle	100	200	300	400	500	600	800	1000
Velocity • fps	2760	2576	2396	2226	2061	1905	1760	1495	1275
Energy • ft-lbs	2351	2045	1772	1528	1311	1120	956	690	502
Taylor KO Index	15.6	14.5	13.5	12.6	11.6	10.7	9.9	8.4	7.2
Path • Inches	-1.5	+1.9	0.0	-7.9	-22.9	-46.1	-79.3	-180.9	-345.1
Wind Drift • Inches	0.0	0.7	2.8	6.4	11.9	19.3	28.8	55.4	93.6

Hornady 139-grain BTSP Interlock (8155)

G1 Ballistic Coefficient = 0.392

Distance • Yards	Muzzle	100	200	300	400	500	600	800	1000
Velocity • fps	2680	2455	2241	2038	1846	1667	1503	1232	1055
Energy • ft-lbs	2216	1860	1550	1282	1052	858	698	468	344
Taylor KO Index	15.1	13.8	12.6	11.5	10.4	9.4	8.5	6.9	5.8
Path • Inches	-1.5	+2.1	0.0	-9.1	-27.4	-56.9	-94.5	-224.8	-447.1
Wind Drift • Inches	0.0	0.9	3.7	8.7	16.2	26.6	40.3	78.8	132.6

7mm-08 Remington

Nosler 120-grain Ballistic Tip (18200)

G1 Ballistic Coefficient = 0.424

Distance • Yards	Muzzle	100	200	300	400	500	600	800	1000
Velocity • fps	3000	2776	2563	2360	2169	1982	1808	1494	1242
Energy • ft-lbs	2399	2055	1752	1485	1252	1048	871	595	411
Taylor KO Index	14.6	13.5	12.5	11.5	10.6	9.6	8.8	7.3	6.0
Path • Inches	-1.5	+1.5	0.0	-6.8	-19.9	-40.4	-69.7	-162.6	-318.5
Wind Drift • Inches	0.0	0.7	2.9	6.8	12.5	20.4	30.7	59.8	102.3

Hornady 139-grain SST (80573)

G1 Ballistic Coefficient = 0.486

Distance • Yards	Muzzle	100	200	300	400	500	600	800	1000
Velocity • fps	2950	2757	2571	2393	2222	2059	1902	1614	1367
Energy • ft-lbs	2686	2345	2040	1768	1524	1308	1117	804	577
Taylor KO Index	16.6	15.5	14.5	13.5	12.5	11.6	10.7	9.1	7.7
Path • Inches	-1.5	+1.5	0.0	-6.8	-19.7	-39.6	-67.8	-154.7	-295.5
Wind Drift • Inches	0.0	0.6	2.6	5.9	10.9	17.7	26.5	51.0	86.5

Hornady 139-grain GMX (80576) ☺

G1 Ballistic Coefficient = 0.486

Distance • Yards	Muzzle	100	200	300	400	500	600	800	1000
Velocity • fps	2910	2718	2534	2358	2189	2026	1871	1587	1344
Energy • ft-lbs	2613	2280	1982	1716	1478	1267	1081	777	558
Taylor KO Index	16.4	15.3	14.3	13.3	12.3	11.4	10.6	8.9	7.6
Path • Inches	-1.5	+1.6	0.0	-7.0	-20.3	-40.9	-69.9	-159.6	-305.1
Wind Drift • Inches	0.0	0.6	2.6	6.1	11.2	18.1	27.1	52.1	88.3

Federal 140-grain Trophy Bonded Tip (P708TT2)

G1 Ballistic Coefficient = 0.431

Distance • Yards	Muzzle	100	200	300	400	500	600	800	1000
Velocity • fps	2800	2590	2390	2200	2010	1840	1677	1390	1170
Energy • ft-lbs	2435	2085	1770	1500	1260	1050	875	601	426
Taylor KO Index	15.9	14.7	13.6	12.5	11.4	10.5	9.5	7.9	6.6
Path • Inches	-1.5	+1.8	0.0	-8.0	-23.2	-46.8	-81.0	-188.8	-369.4
Wind Drift • Inches	0.0	0.8	3.1	7.3	13.6	22.1	33.4	64.9	110.4

.280 Remington

Hornady 139-grain SST (81583)

G1 Ballistic Coefficient = 0.486

Distance • Yards	Muzzle	100	200	300	400	500	600	800	1000
Velocity • fps	3090	2890	2699	2516	2341	2172	2010	1710	1447
Energy • ft-lbs	2946	2578	2249	1954	1691	1456	1248	903	647
Taylor KO Index	17.4	16.3	15.2	14.2	13.2	12.2	11.3	9.6	8.2
Path • Inches	-1.5	+1.3	0.0	-6.1	-17.7	-35.7	-61.0	-139.1	-265.2
Wind Drift • Inches	0.0	0.6	2.4	5.6	10.2	16.6	24.8	47.6	80.6

Hornady 139-grain GMX (81586) ☺

G1 Ballistic Coefficient = 0.486

Distance • Yards	Muzzle	100	200	300	400	500	600	800	1000
Velocity • fps	3070	2871	2681	2499	2324	2156	1995	1696	1435
Energy • ft-lbs	2908	2544	2218	1927	1666	1434	1229	888	636
Taylor KO Index	17.3	16.2	15.1	14.1	13.1	12.2	11.3	9.6	8.1
Path • Inches	-1.5	+1.4	0.0	-6.2	-18.0	-36.2	-61.9	-141.2	-269.2
Wind Drift • Inches	0.0	0.6	2.4	5.6	10.3	16.7	25.0	48.0	81.4

Federal 140-grain Trophy Bonded Tip (P280TT2)

G1 Ballistic Coefficient = 0.432

Distance • Yards	Muzzle	100	200	300	400	500	600	800	1000
Velocity • fps	2950	2730	2520	2330	2140	1960	1790	1484	1239
Energy • ft-lbs	2705	2320	1980	1680	1420	1190	996	685	477
Taylor KO Index	16.8	15.4	14.3	13.2	12.2	11.1	10.2	8.4	7.0
Path • Inches	-1.5	+1.6	0.0	-7.0	-28.6	-41.5	-71.8	-166.9	-325.9
Wind Drift • Inches	0.0	0.7	2.9	6.8	12.5	20.4	30.7	59.8	102.1

7mm Remington Magnum

Federal 110-grain Barnes Triple-Shock X-Bullet (P7RP) ☺

G1 Ballistic Coefficient = 0.429

Distance • Yards	Muzzle	100	200	300	400	500	600	800	1000
Velocity • fps	3500	3200	2920	2650	2400	2170	1948	1551	1240
Energy • ft-lbs	2990	2500	2075	1720	1410	1145	927	588	375
Taylor KO Index	15.6	14.3	13.0	11.8	10.7	9.7	8.7	6.9	5.5
Path • Inches	-1.5	+0.9	0.0	-5.1	-15.0	-31.2	-54.2	-131.3	-266.9
Wind Drift • Inches	0.0	0.7	2.9	6.8	12.6	20.6	31.2	61.9	108.2

Hornady 139-grain SST (80593)

G1 Ballistic Coefficient = 0.486

Distance • Yards	Muzzle	100	200	300	400	500	600	800	1000
Velocity • fps	3240	3033	2836	2648	2467	2293	2126	1814	1537
Energy • ft-lbs	3239	2839	2482	2163	1877	1622	1396	1016	729
Taylor KO Index	18.3	17.1	16.0	14.9	13.9	12.9	12.0	10.2	8.7
Path • Inches	-1.5	+1.1	0.0	-5.5	-15.9	-32.1	-54.8	-124.8	-237.5
Wind Drift • Inches	0.0	0.6	2.2	5.2	9.6	15.5	23.1	44.3	75.0

Hornady 139-grain GMX 80592) ☺

G1 Ballistic Coefficient = 0.486

Distance • Yards	Muzzle	100	200	300	400	500	600	800	1000
Velocity • fps	3190	2986	2791	2604	2425	2253	2088	1780	1507
Energy • ft-lbs	3140	2751	2403	2092	1814	1566	1345	978	701
Taylor KO Index	18.0	16.8	15.7	14.7	13.7	12.7	11.8	10.0	8.5
Path • Inches	-1.5	+1.2	0.0	-5.7	-16.5	-33.2	-56.8	-129.3	-246.2
Wind Drift • Inches	0.0	0.6	2.3	5.3	9.8	15.8	23.6	45.3	76.8

Remington 140-grain Solid Copper Tipped (PCS7MMA) ☺

G1 Ballistic Coefficient = 0.468

Distance • Yards	Muzzle	100	200	300	400	500	600	800	1000
Velocity • fps	3175	2964	2762	2570	2385	2208	2039	1725	1450
Energy • ft-lbs	3133	2730	2372	2053	1768	1516	1293	925	654
Taylor KO Index	18.0	16.8	15.7	14.6	13.5	12.5	11.6	9.8	8.2
Path • Inches	-1.5	+1.2	0.0	-5.8	-16.9	-34.0	-58.4	-133.7	-256.2
Wind Drift • Inches	0.0	0.6	2.4	5.6	10.3	16.7	24.9	48.0	81.6

Remington 140-grain AccuTip Boat Tail (PRA7MMRA)

G1 Ballistic Coefficient = 0.486

Distance • Yards	Muzzle	100	200	300	400	500	600	800	1000
Velocity • fps	3175	2971	2777	2591	2412	2241	2076	1769	1498
Energy • ft-lbs	3133	2744	2397	2086	1808	1560	1340	973	698
Taylor KO Index	18.0	16.9	15.8	14.7	13.7	12.7	11.8	10.0	8.5
Path • Inches	-1.5	+1.2	0.0	-5.7	-16.7	-33.6	-57.4	-130.7	-248.9
Wind Drift • Inches	0.0	0.6	2.3	5.4	9.9	15.9	23.8	45.7	77.3

Federal 140-grain Trophy Bonded Tip (P7RTT2)

G1 Ballistic Coefficient = 0.429

Distance • Yards	Muzzle	100	200	300	400	500	600	800	1000
Velocity • fps	3150	2920	2710	2500	2300	2110	1931	1604	1329
Energy • ft-lbs	3085	2655	2275	1940	1645	1390	1160	800	549
Taylor KO Index	17.9	16.6	15.4	14.2	13.1	12.0	11.0	9.1	7.5
Path • Inches	-1.5	+1.3	0.0	-6.1	-17.6	-35.9	-62.0	-144.0	-280.8
Wind Drift • Inches	0.0	0.6	2.7	6.2	11.5	18.7	28.1	54.6	93.6

Winchester 140-grain E-Tip (P7RTT2) ☺

G1 Ballistic Coefficient = 0.498

Distance • Yards	Muzzle	100	200	300	400	500	600	800	1000
Velocity • fps	3100	2905	2718	2538	2366	2200	2041	1745	1483
Energy • ft-lbs	2988	2623	2296	2003	1740	1505	1295	946	683
Taylor KO Index	17.6	16.5	15.4	14.4	13.4	12.5	11.6	9.9	8.4
Path • Inches	-1.5	+1.3	0.0	-6.0	-17.5	-35.1	-60.0	-136.1	-258.4
Wind Drift • Inches	0.0	0.6	2.3	5.4	9.9	16.0	23.9	45.3	77.5

Winchester 150-grain Power Point Bonded (X7MMR1BP)

G1 Ballistic Coefficient = 0.393

Distance • Yards	Muzzle	100	200	300	400	500	600	800	1000
Velocity • fps	3090	2844	2612	2381	2181	1981	1794	1460	1201
Energy • ft-lbs	3180	2694	2272	1904	1584	1307	1072	710	481
Taylor KO Index	18.8	17.3	15.9	14.5	13.3	12.1	10.9	8.9	7.3
Path • Inches	-1.5	+1.4	0.0	-6.5	-19.1	-39.1	-67.9	-160.5	-319.2
Wind Drift • Inches	0.0	0.7	3.0	7.0	13.1	21.4	32.3	63.5	109.4

Hornady 154-grain SST (8061)

G1 Ballistic Coefficient = 0.525

Distance • Yards	Muzzle	100	200	300	400	500	600	800	1000
Velocity • fps	3100	2914	2736	2565	2401	2242	2089	1803	1546
Energy • ft-lbs	3286	2904	2560	2250	1970	1718	1493	1112	818
Taylor KO Index	19.4	18.2	17.1	16.0	15.0	14.0	13.1	11.3	9.7
Path • Inches	-1.5	+1.3	0.0	-5.9	-17.2	-34.5	-58.7	-132.2	-249.0
Wind Drift • Inches	0.0	0.5	2.2	5.1	9.3	15.1	22.4	42.8	72.0

Federal 160-grain Trophy Bonded Tip (P7RTT1)

G1 Ballistic Coefficient = 0.520

Distance • Yards	Muzzle	100	200	300	400	500	600	800	1000
Velocity • fps	2900	2720	2550	2380	2220	2070	1923	1650	1412
Energy • ft-lbs	2990	2630	2310	2015	1755	1525	1314	968	709
Taylor KO Index	18.8	17.7	16.6	15.4	14.4	13.4	12.5	10.7	9.2
Path • Inches	-1.5	+1.6	0.0	-6.9	-20.0	-40.2	-68.4	-154.7	-292.5
Wind Drift • Inches	0.0	0.6	2.4	5.6	10.4	16.8	25.0	47.9	80.8

Hornady 162-grain SST (80633)

G1 Ballistic Coefficient = 0.549

Distance •Yards	Muzzle	100	200	300	400	500	600	800	1000
Velocity • fps	3030	2855	2688	2525	2370	2219	2073	1800	1554
Energy • ft-lbs	3302	2933	2598	2295	2020	1772	1546	1166	869
Taylor KO Index	19.9	18.8	17.7	16.6	15.6	14.6	13.6	11.8	10.2
Path • Inches	-1.5	+1.4	0.0	-6.2	-17.9	-35.7	-60.7	-136.1	-254.7
Wind Drift • Inches	0.0	0.5	2.2	5.0	9.2	14.8	22.0	41.8	70.1

7mm Winchester Short Magnum

Winchester 140-grain E-Tip (S7SET) ☺

G1 Ballistic Coefficient = 0.498

Distance • Yards	Muzzle	100	200	300	400	500	600	800	1000
Velocity • fps	3150	2952	2763	2582	2408	2241	2080	1926	1513
Energy • ft-lbs	3085	2710	2374	2073	1803	1561	1345	985	712
Taylor KO Index	17.9	16.8	15.7	14.7	13.7	12.7	11.8	10.9	8.6
Path • Inches	-1.5	+1.2	0.0	-5.8	-16.8	-33.9	-57.8	-131.3	-249.0
Wind Drift • Inches	0.0	0.6	2.3	5.3	9.7	15.7	23.4	44.8	75.6

Federal 140-grain Trophy Bonded Tip (P7WSMTT2)

G1 Ballistic Coefficient = 0.429

Distance • Yards	Muzzle	100	200	300	400	500	600	800	1000
Velocity • fps	3200	2970	2750	2540	2340	2150	1969	1636	1355
Energy • ft-lbs	3185	2740	2370	2010	1705	1440	1205	832	571
Taylor KO Index	18.2	16.9	15.6	14.4	13.3	12.2	11.2	9.3	7.7
Path • Inches	-1.5	+1.2	0.0	-5.8	-17.0	-34.7	-59.8	-138.8	-270.5
Wind Drift • Inches	0.0	0.6	2.6	6.1	11.2	18.3	27.5	53.3	91.4

Winchester 150-grain Power Max Bonded (X7WSMBP)

G1 Ballistic Coefficient = 0.393

Distance • Yards	Muzzle	100	200	300	400	500	600	800	1000
Velocity • fps	3200	2948	2710	2484	2270	2066	1873	1526	1248
Energy • ft-lbs	3410	2894	2446	2056	1716	1421	1169	776	520
Taylor KO Index	19.5	17.9	16.5	15.1	13.9	12.6	11.4	9.3	7.6
Path • Inches	-1.5	+1.3	0.0	-6.0	-17.6	-36.1	-62.6	-147.9	-293.6
Wind Drift • Inches	0.0	0.7	2.9	6.7	12.5	20.3	30.7	60.2	104.0

7mm Remington SAUM

Nosler 150-grain Partition (16030)

G1 Ballistic Coefficient = 0.456

Distance • Yards	Muzzle	100	200	300	400	500	600	800	1000
Velocity • fps	3000	2791	2592	2402	2219	2046	1880	1577	1322
Energy • ft-lbs	2997	2595	2238	1921	1641	1394	1178	829	583
Taylor KO Index	18.3	17.0	15.8	14.6	13.5	12.5	11.4	9.6	8.0
Path • Inches	-1.5	+1.5	0.0	-6.7	-19.4	-39.1	-67.2	-154.8	-299.0
Wind Drift • Inches	0.0	0.6	2.7	6.2	11.5	18.7	28.0	54.2	92.2

7mm Remington Ultra Mag.

Nosler 160-grain Partition (16030)

G1 Ballistic Coefficient = 0.456

Distance • Yards	Muzzle	100	200	300	400	500	600	800	1000
Velocity • fps	3225	3015	2813	2621	2437	2260	2092	1777	1499
Energy • ft-lbs	3695	3228	2812	2441	2110	1815	1555	1122	798
Taylor KO Index	20.9	19.6	18.3	17.0	15.8	14.7	13.6	11.5	9.7
Path • Inches	-1.5	+1.2	0.0	-5.6	-16.2	-32.7	-56.0	-127.9	-244.2
Wind Drift • Inches	0.0	0.6	2.3	5.4	9.9	16.0	23.9	46.0	78.0

7mm Weatherby Magnum

Weatherby 120-grain Barnes TTSX (B7MM120TTSX) ☺

G1 Ballistic Coefficient = 0.370

Distance • Yards	Muzzle	100	200	300	400	500	600	800	1000
Velocity • fps	3430	3148	2884	2635	2399	2178	1966	1585	1278
Energy • ft-lbs	3136	2841	2216	1850	1534	1262	1030	670	435
Taylor KO Index	16.7	15.3	14.0	12.8	11.7	10.6	9.6	7.7	6.2
Path • Inches	-1.5	+1.0	0.0	-5.2	-15.4	-31.7	-55.3	-131.8	-264.5
Wind Drift • Inches	0.0	0.7	2.8	6.6	12.2	19.9	30.0	59.1	102.8

7mm STW

Federal 160-grain Trophy Bonded Tip (P7STWTT1)

G1 Ballistic Coefficient = 0.524

Distance • Yards	Muzzle	100	200	300	400	500	600	800	1000
Velocity • fps	3100	2910	2730	2560	2390	2240	2088	1801	1544
Energy • ft-lbs	3415	3015	2655	2330	2035	1775	1549	1153	847
Taylor KO Index	20.1	18.9	17.7	16.6	15.5	14.5	13.6	11.7	10.0
Path • Inches	-1.5	+1.3	0.0	-6.0	-17.2	-34.6	-58.7	-132.4	-249.3
Wind Drift • Inches	0.0	0.5	2.2	5.1	9.4	15.1	22.5	42.9	72.2

.30 M1 Carbine

Sellier & Bellot 110-grain SP (30B)

G1 Ballistic Coefficient = 0.168

Distance • Yards	Muzzle	100	200	300	400	500	600	800	1000
Velocity • fps	1990	1570	1241	1039	926	945	779	670	581
Energy • ft-lbs	968	602	376	264	209	174	148	110	82
Taylor KO Index	9.6	7.6	6.0	5.0	4.5	4.1	3.8	3.2	2.8
Path • Inches	-1.5	+6.4	0.0	-29.1	-90.2	-191.9	-342.3	-825.2	-1622
Wind Drift • Inches	0.0	3.4	14.8	35.2	62.8	95.9	134.6	228.2	345.6

Sellier & Bellot 110-grain FMJ (V332652U)

G1 Ballistic Coefficient = 0.155

Distance • Yards	Muzzle	100	200	300	400	500	600	800	1000
Velocity • fps	2024	1567	1217	1015	903	821	754	642	549
Energy • ft-lbs	1001	600	362	252	199	165	139	101	74
Taylor KO Index	9.8	7.6	5.9	4.9	4.4	4.0	3.6	3.1	2.7
Path • Inches	-1.5	+6.5	0.0	-30.4	-93.7	-200.0	-358.0	-869.4	-1724
Wind Drift • Inches	0.0	3.6	16.0	37.8	67.1	102.4	143.6	244.0	371.2

Sellier & Bellot 110-grain FMJ (30A)

G1 Ballistic Coefficient = 0.184

Distance • Yards	Muzzle	100	200	300	400	500	600	800	1000
Velocity • fps	1990	1604	1290	1080	960	878	812	706	619
Energy • ft-lbs	968	628	407	285	225	188	161	122	94
Taylor KO Index	9.6	7.8	6.2	5.2	4.6	4.2	3.9	3.4	3.0
Path • Inches	-1.5	+6.1	0.0	-27.1	-84.0	-178.4	-318.1	-764.1	-1492
Wind Drift • Inches	0.0	3.0	13.3	31.8	57.4	88.5	124.6	211.5	319.3

7.62x39 Russian

Sellier & Bellot 123-grain SP (V332252U)

G1 Ballistic Coefficient = 0.273

Distance • Yards	Muzzle	100	200	300	400	500	600	800	1000
Velocity • fps	2437	2135	1855	1601	1381	1203	1076	927	830
Energy • ft-lbs	1622	1245	940	701	521	395	316	235	188
Taylor KO Index	13.2	11.6	10.0	8.7	7.5	6.5	5.8	5.0	4.5
Path • Inches	-1.5	+3.1	0.0	-13.2	-40.2	-85.5	-154.8	-388.8	-784.8
Wind Drift • Inches	0.0	1.5	6.4	15.4	29.2	48.6	73.6	136.7	214.2

Sellier & Bellot 123-grain FMJ (V322242U)

G1 Ballistic Coefficient = 0.192

Distance • Yards	Muzzle	100	200	300	400	500	600	800	1000
Velocity • fps	2421	1999	1627	1319	1104	979	895	773	678
Energy • ft-lbs	1601	1092	723	475	333	262	219	163	126
Taylor KO Index	13.1	10.8	8.8	7.1	6.0	5.8	4.8	4.2	3.7
Path • Inches	-1.5	+3.7	0.0	-17.0	-54.1	-119.7	-221.5	-562.7	-1138
Wind Drift • Inches	0.0	2.2	9.7	24.0	46.2	75.4	110.2	194.0	296.9

Hornady 123-grain A-MAX (8078)

G1 Ballistic Coefficient = 0.270

Distance • Yards	Muzzle	100	200	300	400	500	600	800	1000
Velocity • fps	2360	2060	1784	1535	1323	1158	1046	908	815
Energy • ft-lbs	1521	1159	869	644	488	366	299	225	182
Taylor KO Index	12.8	11.1	9.7	8.3	7.2	6.3	5.7	4.9	4.4
Path • Inches	-1.5	+3.4	0.0	-14.4	-43.6	-92.8	-167.8	-418.5	-838.0
Wind Drift • Inches	0.0	1.6	6.8	16.3	31.0	51.4	77.2	141.4	219.9

Cor-Bon 123-grain DPX (DPX762x39123/20)

G1 Ballistic Coefficient = 0.270

Distance • Yards	Muzzle	100	200	300	400	500	600	800	1000
Velocity • fps	2300	2204	1733	1491	1288	1133	1028	898	807
Energy • ft-lbs	1445	1097	821	608	453	351	289	220	178
Taylor KO Index	12.4	11.9	9.4	8.1	7.0	6.1	5.6	4.9	4.4
Path • Inches	-1.5	+3.6	0.0	-15.3	-46.3	-98.3	-177.4	-439.4	-874.2
Wind Drift • Inches	0.0	1.6	7.0	16.9	32.1	53.0	79.2	143.7	222.3

Remington 125-grain Pointed Soft Point (R762391)

G1 Ballistic Coefficient = 0.267

Distance • Yards	Muzzle	100	200	300	400	500	600	800	1000
Velocity • fps	2365	2062	1783	1533	1320	1154	1041	904	811
Energy • ft-lbs	1552	1180	882	652	483	370	301	227	183
Taylor KO Index	13.0	11.3	9.8	8.4	7.3	6.3	5.7	5.0	4.5
Path • Inches	-1.5	+3.4	0.0	-14.4	-43.7	-93.2	-168.7	-421.3	-844.3
Wind Drift • Inches	0.0	1.6	6.8	16.5	31.4	52.0	78.0	142.9	222.0

.30-30 Winchester

Winchester 150-grain Power Max Bonded (X30306BP)

G1 Ballistic Coefficient = 0.224

Distance • Yards	Muzzle	100	200	300	400	500	600	800	1000
Velocity • fps	2390	2028	1702	1420	1198	1052	959	834	741
Energy • ft-lbs	1902	1370	965	672	478	368	306	232	183
Taylor KO Index	15.8	13.4	11.2	9.4	7.9	6.9	6.3	5.5	4.9
Path • Inches	-1.5	+3.5	0.0	-15.7	-48.7	-105.9	-194.5	-491.3	-988.9
Wind Drift • Inches	0.0	1.9	8.2	20.1	38.6	63.8	94.4	168.9	259.6

Federal 150-grain Barnes Triple-Shock X-Bullet (PSC3030WA) ☺

G1 Ballistic Coefficient = 0.185

Distance • Yards	Muzzle	100	200	300	400	500	600	800	1000
Velocity • fps	2220	1800	1450	1180	1020	920	848	734	643
Energy • ft-lbs	1640	1085	695	460	345	280	240	180	138
Taylor KO Index	14.7	11.9	9.6	7.8	6.7	6.1	5.6	4.8	4.2
Path • Inches	-1.5	+4.7	0.0	-21.7	-68.6	-147.8	-267.8	-662.1	-1317
Wind Drift • Inches	0.0	2.6	11.5	28.2	52.3	83.7	119.7	206.5	313.4

Remington 150-grain Copper Solid Tip (PSC3030WA) ☺

G1 Ballistic Coefficient = 0.186

Distance • Yards	Muzzle	100	200	300	400	500	600	800	1000
Velocity • fps	2200	1806	1448	1185	1022	924	852	739	648
Energy • ft-lbs	1641	1066	698	468	348	284	242	182	140
Taylor KO Index	14.5	11.9	9.6	7.8	6.7	6.1	5.6	4.9	4.3
Path • Inches	-1.5	+5.2	0.0	-21.8	-68.6	-149.0	-267.9	-660.3	-1310
Wind Drift • Inches	0.0	2.6	11.4	28.0	52.3	82.8	118.4	204.1	309.6

.308 Winchester

Nosler 125-grain Ballistic Tip (23230S308ETA

G1 Ballistic Coefficient = 0.366

Distance • Yards	Muzzle	100	200	300	400	500	600	800	1000
Velocity • fps	3175	2907	2653	2414	2188	1974	1774	1422	1160
Energy • ft-lbs	2798	2345	1954	1617	1328	1082	874	561	374
Taylor KO Index	17.5	16.0	14.6	13.3	12.0	10.9	9.8	7.8	6.4
Path • Inches	-1.5	+1.3	0.0	-6.3	-18.5	-38.0	-66.5	-159.5	-322.1
Wind Drift • Inches	0.0	0.8	3.1	7.4	13.7	22.5	34.1	67.4	116.8

Nosler 150-grain AccuBond (23201)

G1 Ballistic Coefficient = 0.435

Distance • Yards	Muzzle	100	200	300	400	500	600	800	1000
Velocity • fps	3025	2805	2596	2397	2206	2025	1852	1540	1282
Energy • ft-lbs	3047	2621	2245	1913	1620	1365	1143	790	548
Taylor KO Index	20.0	18.5	17.1	15.8	14.6	13.4	12.2	10.2	8.5
Path • Inches	-1.5	+1.5	0.0	-6.6	-19.3	-39.2	-67.5	-156.7	-305.2
Wind Drift • Inches	0.0	0.7	2.8	6.5	12.0	19.5	29.3	57.0	97.4

Hornady 150-grain SST (80933)

G1 Ballistic Coefficient = 0.332

Distance • Yards	Muzzle	100	200	300	400	500	600	800	1000
Velocity • fps	3000	2772	2555	2348	1963	1744	1543	1220	1026
Energy • ft-lbs	2997	2458	2000	1611	1284	1013	794	495	351
Taylor KO Index	19.6	18.3	16.9	15.5	13.0	11.5	10.2	8.1	6.8
Path • Inches	-1.5	+1.6	0.0	-7.4	-22.1	-45.8	-81.0	-199.4	-411.6
Wind Drift • Inches	0.0	0.9	3.8	8.9	16.7	27.7	42.3	84.4	144.4

Hornady 150-grain GMX (8094) ☺

G1 Ballistic Coefficient = 0.280

Distance • Yards	Muzzle	100	200	300	400	500	600	800	1000
Velocity • fps	2940	2715	2500	2296	2101	1519	1316	1048	914
Energy • ft-lbs	2878	2270	1767	1356	1025	768	577	366	278
Taylor KO Index	19.4	17.9	16.5	15.2	13.9	10.0	8.7	6.9	6.0
Path • Inches	-1.5	+1.8	0.0	-8.4	-25.4	-53.8	-97.4	-250.7	-529.9
Wind Drift • Inches	0.0	1.1	4.7	11.2	21.3	35.8	55.2	110.2	182.9

Winchester 150-grain E-Tip (S308ETA) ☺

G1 Ballistic Coefficient = 0.469

Distance • Yards	Muzzle	100	200	300	400	500	600	800	1000
Velocity • fps	2810	2616	2430	2251	2080	1917	1763	1483	1255
Energy • ft-lbs	2629	2279	1966	1688	1441	1224	1035	733	524
Taylor KO Index	18.5	17.3	16.0	14.9	13.7	12.7	11.6	9.8	8.3
Path • Inches	-1.5	+1.8	0.0	-7.7	-22.3	-44.9	-77.0	-176.9	-340.6
Wind Drift • Inches	0.0	0.7	2.8	6.6	12.2	19.9	29.8	57.6	97.7

Remington 150-grain Copper Solid Tipped (PCS308WA) ☺

G1 Ballistic Coefficient = 0.400

Distance • Yards	Muzzle	100	200	300	400	500	600	800	1000
Velocity • fps	2820	2593	2376	2171	1975	1791	1620	1324	1114
Energy • ft-lbs	2648	2238	1881	1569	1299	1068	874	584	414
Taylor KO Index	18.6	17.1	15.7	14.3	13.0	11.8	10.7	8.7	7.4
Path • Inches	-1.5	+2.0	0.0	-8.0	-23.4	-47.8	-83.0	-196.4	-389.6
Wind Drift • Inches	0.0	0.8	3.4	7.9	14.7	24.0	36.3	71.1	121.1

Sellier & Bellot 150-grain FMJ (308A)

G1 Ballistic Coefficient = 0.456

Distance • Yards	Muzzle	100	200	300	400	500	600	800	1000
Velocity • fps	2820	2620	2429	2245	2070	1903	1745	1460	1232
Energy • ft-lbs	2649	2287	1965	1680	1427	1206	1014	711	506
Taylor KO Index	18.6	17.3	16.0	14.8	13.7	12.6	11.5	9.6	8.1
Path • Inches	-1.5	+1.8	0.0	-7.7	-22.3	-45.0	-77.4	-178.7	-345.8
Wind Drift • Inches	0.0	0.7	2.9	6.8	12.6	20.5	30.7	59.5	101.0

Hornady 155 Palma Match (8095PM)

G1 Ballistic Coefficient = 0.435

Distance • Yards	Muzzle	100	200	300	400	500	600	800	1000
Velocity • fps	2850	2639	2438	2245	2062	1887	1723	1430	1200
Energy • ft-lbs	2795	2397	2045	1735	1463	1225	1022	704	496
Taylor KO Index	19.4	18.0	16.6	15.3	14.1	12.9	11.8	9.8	8.2
Path • Inches	-1.5	+1.8	0.0	-7.6	-22.1	-44.9	-77.4	-180.0	-351.4
Wind Drift • Inches	0.0	0.7	3.0	7.1	13.1	21.3	32.1	62.4	106.3

Lapua 155-grain Scenar (4317073)

G1 Ballistic Coefficient = 0.452

Distance • Yards	Muzzle	100	200	300	400	500	600	800	1000
Velocity • fps	2820	2621	2428	2243	2064	1895	1735	1451	1182
Energy • ft-lbs	2725	2354	2020	1723	1466	1237	1031	725	478
Taylor KO Index	19.2	17.9	16.6	15.3	14.1	12.9	11.8	9.9	8.1
Path • Inches	-1.5	+1.8	0.0	-7.7	-22.4	-45.2	-77.7	-179.8	-348.4
Wind Drift • Inches	0.0	0.7	2.9	6.9	12.7	20.7	31.1	60.2	102.3

Hornady 165-grain SST (80983)

G1 Ballistic Coefficient = 0.447

Distance • Yards	Muzzle	100	200	300	400	500	600	800	1000
Velocity • fps	2840	2635	2439	2252	2079	1902	1741	1452	1222
Energy • ft-lbs	2955	2544	2180	1858	1574	1325	1111	773	547
Taylor KO Index	20.6	19.1	18.1	16.3	15.1	13.8	12.6	10.5	8.9
Path • Inches	-1.5	+1.8	0.0	-7.6	-22.1	-44.7	-76.9	-178.2	-345.9
Wind Drift • Inches	0.0	0.7	3.0	6.9	12.7	20.7	31.2	60.5	102.8

Nosler 165-grain Partition (23205)

G1 Ballistic Coefficient = 0.410

Distance • Yards	Muzzle	100	200	300	400	500	600	800	1000
Velocity • fps	2800	2579	2368	2168	1978	1798	1629	1339	1127
Energy • ft-lbs	2872	2436	2054	1721	1433	1185	973	657	466
Taylor KO Index	20.3	18.7	17.2	15.7	14.4	13.1	11.8	9.7	8.2
Path • Inches	-1.5	+1.9	0.0	-8.1	-23.6	-48.0	-83.2	-195.9	-386.8
Wind Drift • Inches	0.0	0.8	3.3	7.7	14.4	23.5	35.6	69.5	118.2

Hornady 165-grain GMX (8099) ☺

G1 Ballistic Coefficient = 0.447

Distance • Yards	Muzzle	100	200	300	400	500	600	800	1000
Velocity • fps	2750	2549	2357	2173	1998	1831	1674	1397	1181
Energy • ft-lbs	2770	2380	2036	1730	1462	1228	1027	715	512
Taylor KO Index	20.0	18.5	17.1	15.8	14.5	13.3	12.2	10.1	8.6
Path • Inches	-1.5	+1.9	0.0	-8.2	-23.8	-48.1	-82.8	-192.0	-373.0
Wind Drift • Inches	0.0	0.7	3.1	7.2	13.4	21.8	32.7	63.5	107.6

Lapua 170-grain Naturalis (N317201)

G1 Ballistic Coefficient = 0.316

Distance • Yards	Muzzle	100	200	300	400	500	600	800	1000
Velocity • fps	2625	2352	2094	1855	1633	1436	1269	1045	924
Energy • ft-lbs	2597	2085	1652	1297	1007	779	608	412	322
Taylor KO Index	19.6	17.6	15.7	13.9	12.2	10.7	9.5	7.8	6.9
Path • Inches	-1.5	+2.4	0.0	-10.4	-30.9	-64.6	-115.2	-286.5	-584.7
Wind Drift • Inches	0.0	1.1	4.8	11.5	21.8	36.2	55.2	107.6	175.4

Lapua 170-grain Lock Base (4317596)

G1 Ballistic Coefficient = 0.432

Distance • Yards	Muzzle	100	200	300	400	500	600	800	1000
Velocity • fps	2820	2636	2454	2274	2107	1947	1795	1518	1287
Energy • ft-lbs	2997	2619	2269	1949	1676	1431	1216	870	625
Taylor KO Index	21.1	19.7	18.4	17.0	15.8	14.6	13.4	11.4	9.6
Path • Inches	-1.5	+1.8	0.0	-7.6	-21.9	-44.0	-75.4	-172.5	-330.5
Wind Drift • Inches	0.0	0.7	2.7	6.4	11.8	19.1	28.7	55.3	93.6

.308 Marlin Express

The .308 Marlin Express is a 2008 development resulting from a joint effort of Marlin and Hornady. Marlin wanted a modern cartridge for its lever-action rifle. The result is a spin-off of the .307 Winchester. Since the only current .307 loading uses the 180-grain Winchester Power Point bullet, it is not suitable for use in tubular magazines, hence a new cartridge designation. Ballistics are said to be similar to the .308, but the only loading available today falls a little short of that. Still, it is a very powerful lever-action cartridge.

Hornady 160-grain FTX (82733)

G1 Ballistic Coefficient = 0.432

Distance • Yards	Muzzle	100	200	300	400	500	600	800	1000
Velocity • fps	2660	2430	2226	2026	1836	1659	1497	1229	1055
Energy • ft-lbs	2513	2111	1761	1457	1197	978	796	536	395
Taylor KO Index	18.7	17.1	15.7	14.3	12.9	11.7	10.5	8.7	7.4
Path • Inches	-1.5	+2.2	0.0	-9.2	-26.9	-55.0	-95.7	-227.4	-451.4
Wind Drift • Inches	0.0	0.9	3.7	8.7	16.2	26.7	40.3	78.8	132.5

.30-06 Springfield

Federal 110-grain Barnes Triple-Shock X-Bullet (13063) ☺

G1 Ballistic Coefficient = 0.331

Distance • Yards	Muzzle	100	200	300	400	500	600	800	1000
Velocity • fps	3400	3090	2800	2520	2270	2030	1804	1413	1134
Energy • ft-lbs	2825	2330	1910	1555	1255	1000	735	488	311
Taylor KO Index	16.5	15.0	13.6	12.2	11.0	9.8	8.7	6.8	5.5
Path • Inches	-1.5	+1.1	0.0	-5.5	-16.5	-34.4	-60.6	-148.2	-306.6
Wind Drift • Inches	0.0	0.8	3.2	7.5	14.0	23.1	35.2	70.4	123.4

Hornady 150-grain SST (81093)

G1 Ballistic Coefficient = 0.415

Distance • Yards	Muzzle	100	200	300	400	500	600	800	1000
Velocity • fps	3080	2848	2627	2417	2216	2025	1845	1519	1256
Energy • ft-lbs	3159	2700	2298	1945	1636	1366	1134	739	526
Taylor KO Index	20.3	18.8	17.3	16.0	14.6	13.4	12.2	10.0	8.3
Path • Inches	-1.5	+1.4	0.0	-6.4	-18.9	-38.4	-66.4	-155.3	-305.2
Wind Drift • Inches	0.0	0.7	2.8	6.7	12.3	20.1	30.3	59.2	101.6

Winchester 150-grain Power Max Bonded (X30061BP)

G1 Ballistic Coefficient = 0.325

Distance • Yards	Muzzle	100	200	300	400	500	600	800	1000
Velocity • fps	2920	2636	2368	2117	1882	1664	1469	1165	995
Energy • ft-lbs	2836	2313	1868	1492	1179	922	719	452	330
Taylor KO Index	19.3	17.4	15.6	14.0	12.4	11.0	9.7	7.7	6.6
Path • Inches	-1.5	+1.8	0.0	-8.0	-23.8	-49.4	-87.7	-217.2	-449.2
Wind Drift • Inches	0.0	1.0	4.0	9.5	17.9	29.6	45.4	90.4	153.2

Sellier & Bellot 150-grain SPCE (V331602U)

G1 Ballistic Coefficient = 0.324

Distance • Yards	Muzzle	100	200	300	400	500	600	800	1000
Velocity • fps	2887	2604	2338	2087	1853	1638	1445	1149	986
Energy • ft-lbs	2777	2259	1821	1452	1145	894	696	440	324
Taylor KO Index	19.1	17.2	15.4	13.8	12.2	10.8	9.5	7.6	6.5
Path • Inches	-1.5	+1.8	0.0	-8.2	-24.4	-50.8	-90.3	-223.8	-462.6
Wind Drift • Inches	0.0	1.0	4.1	9.7	18.3	30.3	46.3	92.4	155.7

Hornady 150-grain GMX (8112) ☺

G1 Ballistic Coefficient = 0.415

Distance • Yards	Muzzle	100	200	300	400	500	600	800	1000
Velocity • fps	3080	2848	2627	2417	2216	2025	1845	1519	1256
Energy • ft-lbs	3159	2700	2298	1945	1636	1366	1134	739	526
Taylor KO Index	20.3	18.8	17.3	16.0	14.6	13.4	12.2	10.0	8.3
Path • Inches	-1.5	+1.4	0.0	-6.4	-18.9	-38.4	-66.4	-155.3	-305.2
Wind Drift • Inches	0.0	0.7	2.8	6.7	12.3	20.1	30.3	59.2	101.6

Remington 150-grain Copper Solid Tipped (PSC3006A) ☺

G1 Ballistic Coefficient = 0.400

Distance • Yards	Muzzle	100	200	300	400	500	600	800	1000
Velocity • fps	2910	2678	2458	2248	2048	1860	1683	1375	1147
Energy • ft-lbs	2820	2388	2012	1683	1397	1152	944	630	438
Taylor KO Index	19.2	17.7	16.2	14.8	13.5	12.3	11.1	9.1	7.6
Path • Inches	-1.5	+1.7	0.0	-7.4	-21.8	-44.5	-77.2	-182.4	-361.8
Wind Drift • Inches	0.0	0.8	3.2	7.8	14.0	22.9	34.6	67.9	116.1

Winchester 150-grain E-Tip (81093) ☺

G1 Ballistic Coefficient = 0.469

Distance • Yards	Muzzle	100	200	300	400	500	600	800	1000
Velocity • fps	2900	2702	2512	2330	2156	1989	1831	1542	1301
Energy • ft-lbs	2801	2431	2102	1809	1548	1318	1117	792	564
Taylor KO Index	19.1	17.8	16.6	15.4	14.2	13.1	12.1	10.2	8.6
Path • Inches	-1.5	+1.6	0.0	-7.2	-20.7	-41.8	-71.6	-164.5	-316.4
Wind Drift • Inches	0.0	0.7	2.7	6.3	11.7	19.0	28.4	54.9	93.2

Hornady 165-grain SST (81153)

G1 Ballistic Coefficient = 0.447

Distance • Yards	Muzzle	100	200	300	400	500	600	800	1000
Velocity • fps	2960	2750	2549	2357	2173	1997	1831	1529	1280
Energy • ft-lbs	3209	2769	2380	2034	1729	1461	1228	856	600
Taylor KO Index	21.5	20.0	18.5	17.1	15.8	14.5	13.3	11.1	9.3
Path • Inches	-1.5	+1.6	0.0	-6.9	-20.1	-40.7	-70.0	-161.8	-313.8
Wind Drift • Inches	0.0	0.7	2.8	6.5	12.0	19.5	29.3	56.8	96.8

Hornady 165-grain GMX (8116) ☺

G1 Ballistic Coefficient = 0.447

Distance • Yards	Muzzle	100	200	300	400	500	600	800	1000
Velocity • fps	2940	2730	2531	2339	2156	1981	1816	1516	1270
Energy • ft-lbs	3166	2731	2346	2004	1703	1438	1203	842	591
Taylor KO Index	21.3	19.8	18.4	17.0	15.7	14.4	13.2	11.0	9.2
Path • Inches	-1.5	+1.6	0.0	-7.0	-20.4	-41.3	-71.1	-164.4	-318.9
Wind Drift • Inches	0.0	0.7	2.8	6.6	12.1	19.7	29.6	57.4	97.8

Remington 165-grain Solid Copper Tipped (PSC3006B) ☺

G1 Ballistic Coefficient = 0.447

Distance • Yards	Muzzle	100	200	300	400	500	600	800	1000
Velocity • fps	2800	2597	2403	2217	2039	1870	1711	1427	1204
Energy • ft-lbs	2872	2470	2115	1800	1523	1281	1073	747	531
Taylor KO Index	20.3	18.9	17.4	16.1	14.8	13.6	12.4	10.4	8.7
Path • Inches	-1.5	+2.1	0.0	-8.2	-23.4	-47.1	-79.4	-184.1	-357.6
Wind Drift • Inches	0.0	0.7	3.0	7.0	13.0	21.2	31.8	61.8	104.9

Sellier & Bellot 168-grain HPBT (V331642U)

G1 Ballistic Coefficient = 0.462

Distance • Yards	Muzzle	100	200	300	400	500	600	800	1000
Velocity • fps	2786	2590	2402	2222	2050	1886	1731	1452	1228
Energy • ft-lbs	2896	2503	2158	1843	1568	1327	1118	787	563
Taylor KO Index	18.4	17.1	15.9	14.7	13.5	12.4	11.4	9.6	8.1
Path • Inches	-1.5	+1.8	0.0	-7.9	-22.8	-46.0	-79.1	-182.2	-351.9
Wind Drift • Inches	0.0	0.7	2.9	6.8	12.6	20.5	30.8	59.6	101.0

Hornady 168-grain A-MAX Match (M1 Garand) (81170)

G1 Ballistic Coefficient = 0.475

Distance • Yards	Muzzle	100	200	300	400	500	600	800	1000
Velocity • fps	2710	2522	2342	2170	2004	1847	1698	1432	1218
Energy • ft-lbs	2739	2373	2046	1756	1499	1272	1076	765	554
Taylor KO Index	20.0	18.9	17.3	16.0	14.8	13.7	12.6	10.6	9.0
Path • Inches	-1.5	+2.3	0.0	-8.6	-24.7	-49.4	-83.1	-190.8	-366.9
Wind Drift • Inches	0.0	0.7	3.0	6.9	12.7	20.7	31.0	59.9	101.1

Federal 180-grain Trophy Bonded Tip (P3006TT4)

G1 Ballistic Coefficient = 0.498

Distance • Yards	Muzzle	100	200	300	400	500	600	800	1000
Velocity • fps	2880	2700	2520	2350	2180	2020	1870	1592	1354
Energy • ft-lbs	3316	2902	2530	2197	1898	1633	1398	1013	733
Taylor KO Index	22.8	21.4	20.0	18.6	17.3	16.0	14.8	12.6	10.7
Path • Inches	-1.5	+1.6	0.0	-7.2	-20.6	-41.5	-70.8	-161.1	-306.8
Wind Drift • Inches	0.0	0.6	2.6	6.0	11.0	17.8	26.7	51.3	86.6

Hornady 180-grain SST (81183)

G1 Ballistic Coefficient = 0.480

Distance • Yards	Muzzle	100	200	300	400	500	600	800	1000
Velocity • fps	2820	2630	2447	2272	2104	1944	1791	1513	1283
Energy • ft-lbs	3178	2764	2393	2063	1769	1509	1282	916	658
Taylor KO Index	22.3	20.8	19.4	18.0	16.7	15.4	14.2	12.0	10.2
Path • Inches	-1.5	+1.8	0.0	-7.6	-21.9	-44.1	-75.5	-172.9	-331.6
Wind Drift • Inches	0.0	0.7	2.8	6.4	11.8	19.2	28.8	55.6	94.1

.300 H & H Magnum

Nosler 150-grain AccuBond (20002)

G1 Ballistic Coefficient = 0.435

Distance • Yards	Muzzle	100	200	300	400	500	600	800	1000
Velocity • fps	3200	2972	2755	2548	2350	2162	1983	1653	1373
Energy • ft-lbs	3410	2941	2527	2162	1840	1557	1310	911	628
Taylor KO Index	21.1	19.6	18.2	16.8	15.5	14.3	13.1	10.9	9.1
Path • Inches	-1.5	+1.2	0.0	-5.8	-17.0	-34.5	-59.4	-137.6	-267.2
Wind Drift • Inches	0.0	0.6	2.6	6.0	11.1	18.0	27.0	52.3	89.6

Nosler 180-grain AccuBond (20043)

G1 Ballistic Coefficient = 0.507

Distance • Yards	Muzzle	100	200	300	400	500	600	800	1000
Velocity • fps	2950	2764	2586	2414	2249	2091	1940	1658	1414
Energy • ft-lbs	3478	3053	2672	2329	2022	1748	1505	1100	799
Taylor KO Index	23.4	21.9	20.5	19.1	17.8	16.6	15.4	13.1	11.2
Path • Inches	-1.5	+1.5	0.0	-6.7	-19.4	-39.0	-66.6	-150.5	-286.3
Wind Drift • Inches	0.0	0.6	2.4	5.7	10.4	16.9	25.2	48.3	81.5

Nosler 180-grain Partition (20063)

G1 Ballistic Coefficient = 0.474

Distance • Yards	Muzzle	100	200	300	400	500	600	800	1000
Velocity • fps	2950	2751	2561	2379	2205	2038	1879	1587	1339
Energy • ft-lbs	3478	3025	2622	2262	1942	1660	1411	1006	717
Taylor KO Index	23.4	21.8	20.3	18.8	17.5	16.1	14.9	12.6	10.6
Path • Inches	-1.5	+1.6	0.0	-6.8	-19.8	-40.0	-68.6	-157.1	-301.3
Wind Drift • Inches	0.0	0.6	2.6	6.1	11.2	18.3	27.3	52.8	89.6

Hornady 180-grain Interbond (8210)

G1 Ballistic Coefficient = 0.480

Distance • Yards	Muzzle	100	200	300	400	500	600	800	1000
Velocity • fps	2870	2678	2493	2316	2146	1984	1829	1547	1309
Energy • ft-lbs	3292	2865	2484	2144	1841	1573	1338	956	685
Taylor KO Index	22.7	21.2	19.7	18.3	17.0	15.7	14.5	12.3	10.4
Path • Inches	-1.5	+1.7	0.0	-7.3	-21.0	-42.4	-72.6	-166.0	-318.2
Wind Drift • Inches	0.0	0.6	2.7	6.3	11.6	18.7	28.1	54.1	91.7

Nosler 180-grain Ballistic Tip (20051)

G1 Ballistic Coefficient = 0.506

Distance • Yards	Muzzle	100	200	300	400	500	600	800	1000
Velocity • fps	2950	2764	2586	2414	2249	2091	1939	1857	1412
Energy • ft-lbs	3478	3053	2672	2329	2022	1748	1502	1098	787
Taylor KO Index	23.4	21.9	20.5	19.1	17.8	16.6	15.4	14.7	11.2
Path • Inches	-1.5	+1.5	0.0	-6.7	-19.4	-39.0	-66.6	-151.1	-286.7
Wind Drift • Inches	0.0	0.6	2.4	5.7	10.4	16.9	25.2	48.4	81.7

Nosler 200-grain AccuBond (20070)

G1 Ballistic Coefficient = 0.588

Distance • Yards	Muzzle	100	200	300	400	500	600	800	1000
Velocity • fps	2750	2596	2448	2304	2165	2032	1903	1662	1448
Energy • ft-lbs	3358	2993	2661	2357	2082	1834	1609	1227	931
Taylor KO Index	24.2	22.8	21.5	20.3	19.1	17.9	16.7	14.6	12.7
Path • Inches	-1.5	+1.8	0.0	-7.6	-21.8	-43.4	-73.5	-163.8	-304.7
Wind Drift • Inches	0.0	0.6	2.3	5.3	9.8	15.4	23.4	44.4	74.1

Nosler 180-grain Partition (20084)

G1 Ballistic Coefficient = 0.482

Distance • Yards	Muzzle	100	200	300	400	500	600	800	1000
Velocity • fps	2750	2563	2383	2211	2046	1890	1741	1492	1251
Energy • ft-lbs	3358	2917	2522	2171	1860	1586	1347	962	695
Taylor KO Index	24.2	22.6	21.0	19.5	18.0	16.6	15.3	13.0	11.0
Path • Inches	-1.5	+1.9	0.0	-8.0	-23.2	-46.6	-79.8	-182.7	-350.5
Wind Drift • Inches	0.0	0.7	2.8	6.6	12.2	19.9	29.8	57.4	97.1

.300 Winchester Short Magnum

Remington 150-grain Core-Lokt Pointed Soft Point (R300WSM1)

G1 Ballistic Coefficient = 0.294

Distance • Yards	Muzzle	100	200	300	400	500	600	800	1000
Velocity • fps	3320	2977	2600	2364	2087	1830	1597	1220	1010
Energy • ft-lbs	3671	2952	2356	1861	1451	1116	849	497	340
Taylor KO Index	21.9	19.6	17.2	15.6	13.8	12.1	10.5	8.1	6.7
Path • Inches	-1.5	+1.2	0.0	-6.2	-18.6	-39.0	-69.9	-177.1	-377.9
Wind Drift • Inches	0.0	0.9	3.8	8.9	16.8	27.9	42.9	87.1	151.4

Winchester 150-grain Power Max Bonded (X300SBP)

G1 Ballistic Coefficient = 0.325

Distance • Yards	Muzzle	100	200	300	400	500	600	800	1000
Velocity • fps	3270	2962	2675	2406	2152	1914	1694	1322	1078
Energy • ft-lbs	3561	2922	2384	1927	1542	1220	956	583	387
Taylor KO Index	21.6	19.5	17.7	15.9	14.2	12.6	11.2	8.7	7.1
Path • Inches	-1.5	+1.2	0.0	-6.1	-18.3	-37.9	-67.2	-165.6	-344.4
Wind Drift • Inches	0.0	0.8	3.4	8.1	15.2	25.0	38.2	76.7	133.6

Federal 165-grain Trophy Bonded Tip (P300WSMTT2)

G1 Ballistic Coefficient = 0.451

Distance • Yards	Muzzle	100	200	300	400	500	600	800	1000
Velocity • fps	3130	2910	2710	2510	2320	2140	1968	1651	1379
Energy • ft-lbs	3590	3110	2680	2305	1970	1675	1419	988	697
Taylor KO Index	22.7	21.1	19.7	18.2	16.8	15.5	14.3	12.0	10.0
Path • Inches	-1.5	+1.3	0.0	-6.0	-17.6	-35.7	-61.4	-141.4	-273.0
Wind Drift • Inches	0.0	0.6	2.6	5.9	11.0	17.8	26.6	51.3	87.9

Federal 165-grain Nosler Partition (P300WSME)

G1 Ballistic Coefficient = 0.412

Distance • Yards	Muzzle	100	200	300	400	500	600	800	1000
Velocity • fps	3120	2880	2660	2450	2240	2050	1866	1535	1267
Energy • ft-lbs	3565	3045	2590	2190	1840	1535	1277	864	588
Taylor KO Index	22.7	20.9	19.3	17.8	16.3	14.9	13.5	11.1	9.2
Path • Inches	-1.5	+1.4	0.0	-6.2	-18.3	-37.4	-64.7	-151.5	-298.0
Wind Drift • Inches	0.0	0.7	2.8	6.6	12.2	19.9	30.0	58.6	100.7

Remington 180-grain AccuTip Boat Tail (PRA300WSMB)

G1 Ballistic Coefficient = 0.480

Distance • Yards	Muzzle	100	200	300	400	500	600	800	1000
Velocity • fps	3010	2812	2622	2440	2265	2097	1937	1641	1386
Energy • ft-lbs	3621	3159	2746	2378	2050	1757	1500	1077	768
Taylor KO Index	23.8	22.3	20.8	19.3	17.9	16.6	15.3	13.0	11.0
Path • Inches	-1.5	+1.4	0.0	-6.5	-18.9	-38.0	-65.1	-148.8	-284.6
Wind Drift • Inches	0.0	0.6	2.5	5.8	10.8	17.5	26.1	50.3	85.3

Remington 180-grain Swift Scirocco Bonded (PRSC300WSMB)

G1 Ballistic Coefficient = 0.507

Distance • Yards	Muzzle	100	200	300	400	500	600	800	1000
Velocity • fps	2980	2793	2614	2442	2276	2116	1964	1680	1432
Energy • ft-lbs	3549	3118	2730	2382	2070	1790	1542	1128	819
Taylor KO Index	23.6	22.1	20.7	19.3	18.0	16.8	15.6	13.3	11.3
Path • Inches	-1.5	+1.5	0.0	-6.6	-19.0	-38.1	-65.0	-147.5	-279.6
Wind Drift • Inches	0.0	0.6	2.4	5.6	10.3	16.6	24.8	47.5	80.3

.300 Winchester Magnum

Winchester 150-grain Power Max Bonded (X30WM1BP)

G1 Ballistic Coefficient = 0.325

Distance • Yards	Muzzle	100	200	300	400	500	600	800	1000
Velocity • fps	3290	2981	2693	2422	2168	1929	1708	1332	1084
Energy • ft-lbs	3605	2959	2415	1954	1565	1239	971	591	391
Taylor KO Index	21.7	19.7	17.8	16.0	14.3	12.7	11.3	8.8	7.2
Path • Inches	-1.5	+1.2	0.0	-6.0	-19.0	-37.4	-66.2	-163.2	-399.4
Wind Drift • Inches	0.0	0.8	3.4	8.0	15.0	24.8	37.8	76.0	132.6

Hornady 150-grain GMX (82012) ☺

G1 Ballistic Coefficient = 0.415

Distance • Yards	Muzzle	100	200	300	400	500	600	800	1000
Velocity • fps	3400	3150	2914	2690	2477	2273	2080	1723	1418
Energy • ft-lbs	3850	3304	2827	2409	2043	1721	1441	989	669
Taylor KO Index	22.4	20.8	19.2	17.8	16.3	15.0	13.7	11.4	9.4
Path • Inches	-1.5	+1.0	0.0	-5.1	-15.0	-30.6	-53.0	-123.5	-241.5
Wind Drift • Inches	0.0	0.6	2.5	5.8	10.8	17.5	26.2	51.0	87.6

Winchester 150-grain E-Tip (S300WMETA) ☺

G1 Ballistic Coefficient = 0.486

Distance • Yards	Muzzle	100	200	300	400	500	600	800	1000
Velocity • fps	3260	3083	2877	2679	2491	2310	2142	1828	1549
Energy • ft-lbs	3539	3088	2687	2329	2011	1728	1528	1114	800
Taylor KO Index	21.5	20.3	19.0	17.7	16.4	15.2	14.1	12.1	10.2
Path • Inches	-1.5	+1.1	0.0	-5.4	-15.9	-32.1	-54.1	-123.1	-234.4
Wind Drift • Inches	0.0	0.5	2.2	5.2	9.5	15.4	22.9	43.9	74.3

Remington 150-grain Copper Solid Tipped (PCS300WA) ☺

G1 Ballistic Coefficient = 0.400

Distance • Yards	Muzzle	100	200	300	400	500	600	800	1000
Velocity • fps	3290	3037	2799	2572	2357	2152	1958	1605	1313
Energy • ft-lbs	3605	3072	2608	2204	1850	1542	1277	858	574
Taylor KO Index	21.7	20.0	18.5	17.0	15.6	14.2	12.9	10.6	8.7
Path • Inches	-1.5	+1.1	0.0	-5.6	-16.4	-33.6	-58.2	-136.8	-270.2
Wind Drift • Inches	0.0	0.7	2.7	6.4	11.7	19.1	28.8	56.4	97.2

Nosler 165-grain Partition (23320)

G1 Ballistic Coefficient = 0.417

Distance • Yards	Muzzle	100	200	300	400	500	600	800	1000
Velocity • fps	3100	2867	2647	2436	2236	2045	1864	1537	1271
Energy • ft-lbs	3521	3011	2567	2174	1832	1532	1274	866	592
Taylor KO Index	22.5	20.8	19.2	17.7	16.2	14.8	13.5	11.2	9.2
Path • Inches	-1.5	+1.4	0.0	-6.3	-18.6	-37.7	-65.2	-152.5	-299.2
Wind Drift • Inches	0.0	0.7	2.8	6.6	12.2	19.8	29.8	58.2	99.9

Federal 165-grain Trophy Bonded Tip (P300WTT2)

G1 Ballistic Coefficient = 0.453

Distance • Yards	Muzzle	100	200	300	400	500	600	800	1000
Velocity • fps	3050	2840	2630	2440	2250	2080	1912	1603	1341
Energy • ft-lbs	3410	2950	2540	2180	1860	1575	1339	941	659
Taylor KO Index	22.1	20.6	19.1	17.7	16.3	15.1	13.9	11.6	9.7
Path • Inches	-1.5	+1.4	0.0	-6.4	-18.7	-37.9	-64.9	-149.7	-289.1
Wind Drift • Inches	0.0	0.6	2.6	6.1	11.3	18.4	27.5	53.3	90.8

Hornady 165-grain GMX (82026) ☺

G1 Ballistic Coefficient = 0.447

Distance • Yards	Muzzle	100	200	300	400	500	600	800	1000
Velocity • fps	3260	3035	2821	2617	2422	2235	2057	1727	1440
Energy • ft-lbs	3893	3373	2915	2505	2148	1830	1550	1093	760
Taylor KO Index	23.7	22.0	20.5	19.0	17.6	16.2	14.9	12.5	10.5
Path • Inches	-1.5	+1.1	0.0	-5.5	-16.1	-32.7	-56.2	-129.5	-250.0
Wind Drift • Inches	0.0	0.6	2.4	5.7	10.5	17.0	25.4	49.1	83.7

Remington 165-grain Copper Solid Tipped (PCS300WB) ☺

G1 Ballistic Coefficient = 0.447

Distance • Yards	Muzzle	100	200	300	400	500	600	800	1000
Velocity • fps	3260	3035	2821	2617	2422	2235	2057	1727	1440
Energy • ft-lbs	3893	3373	2915	2505	2148	1830	1550	1093	760
Taylor KO Index	23.7	22.0	20.5	19.0	17.6	16.2	14.9	12.5	10.5
Path • Inches	-1.5	+1.1	0.0	-5.5	-16.1	-32.7	-56.2	-129.5	-250.0
Wind Drift • Inches	0.0	0.6	2.4	5.7	10.5	17.0	25.4	49.1	83.7

Remington 180-grain Core-Lokt Pointed Soft Point (R300W2)

G1 Ballistic Coefficient = 0.383

Distance • Yards	Muzzle	100	200	300	400	500	600	800	1000
Velocity • fps	2960	2715	2482	2262	2052	1856	1674	1355	1126
Energy • ft-lbs	3501	2945	2463	2044	1683	1375	1120	734	507
Taylor KO Index	23.4	21.5	19.7	17.9	16.3	14.7	13.3	10.7	8.9
Path • Inches	-1.5	+1.7	0.0	-7.4	-21.3	-43.7	-76.1	-181.3	-363.0
Wind Drift • Inches	0.0	0.8	3.3	7.7	14.4	23.6	35.7	70.3	120.6

Winchester 180-grain Power-Point (X30WM2)

G1 Ballistic Coefficient = 0.438

Distance • Yards	Muzzle	100	200	300	400	500	600	800	1000
Velocity • fps	2960	2745	2540	2340	2157	1979	1811	1506	1258
Energy • ft-lbs	3501	3011	2578	2196	1859	1565	1311	907	633
Taylor KO Index	23.4	21.7	20.1	18.5	17.1	15.7	14.3	11.9	10.0
Path • Inches	-1.5	+1.6	0.0	-7.0	-20.3	-41.0	-70.7	-164.1	-319.4
Wind Drift • Inches	0.0	0.7	2.8	6.6	12.3	20.0	30.0	58.4	99.6

Winchester 180-grain Power Max Bonded (X30WM2)

G1 Ballistic Coefficient = 0.394

Distance • Yards	Muzzle	100	200	300	400	500	600	800	1000
Velocity • fps	2960	2722	2496	2281	2077	1884	1703	1387	1152
Energy • ft-lbs	3501	2961	2490	2080	1724	1419	1160	769	530
Taylor KO Index	23.4	21.6	19.8	18.1	16.4	14.9	13.5	11.0	9.1
Path • Inches	-1.5	+1.6	0.0	-7.2	-21.1	-43.1	-74.9	-177.3	-352.7
Wind Drift • Inches	0.0	0.8	3.2	7.5	13.9	22.7	34.4	67.6	115.9

Sellier & Bellot 180-grain PTS (V332552U)

G1 Ballistic Coefficient = 0.480

Distance • Yards	Muzzle	100	200	300	400	500	600	800	1000
Velocity • fps	2936	2741	2554	2374	2202	2037	1880	1591	1345
Energy • ft-lbs	3446	3003	2607	2254	1939	1659	1413	1012	723
Taylor KO Index	23.3	21.7	20.2	18.8	17.4	16.1	14.9	12.6	10.7
Path • Inches	-1.5	+1.6	0.0	-6.9	-20.0	-40.2	-68.9	-157.6	-301.7
Wind Drift • Inches	0.0	0.6	2.6	6.1	11.2	18.1	27.1	52.2	88.6

Hornady 180-grain SST (82193)

G1 Ballistic Coefficient = 0.480

Distance • Yards	Muzzle	100	200	300	400	500	600	800	1000
Velocity • fps	3130	2927	2732	2546	2366	2195	2029	1724	1456
Energy • ft-lbs	3917	3424	2953	2589	2238	1925	1646	1188	847
Taylor KO Index	24.8	23.2	21.6	20.2	18.7	17.4	16.1	13.7	11.5
Path • Inches	-1.5	+1.3	0.0	-5.9	-17.3	-34.8	-59.6	-136.0	-259.8
Wind Drift • Inches	0.0	0.6	2.4	5.6	10.2	16.5	24.7	47.4	80.4

.300 RCM (Ruger Compact Magnum)

This is another example of the latest trend in magnum cartridge design, the nonbelted magnum. These cartridges generally have base diameters the same as the belt diameters found on the classic belted magnums. It is very similar in both dimensions and proportions to the Winchester Short Magnum, but they are definitely NOT Interchangeable.

Hornady 150-grain SST (82231)

G1 Ballistic Coefficient = 0.415

Distance • Yards	Muzzle	100	200	300	400	500	600	800	1000
Velocity • fps	3310	3065	2833	2613	2404	2204	2014	1665	1370
Energy • ft-lbs	3648	3128	2673	2274	1924	1618	1351	924	626
Taylor KO Index	21.8	20.2	18.7	17.2	15.9	14.5	13.3	11.0	9.0
Path • Inches	-1.5	+1.1	0.0	-5.4	-16.0	-32.6	-56.3	-131.4	-257.2
Wind Drift • Inches	0.0	0.6	2.6	6.0	11.2	18.2	27.3	53.1	91.2

Hornady 150-grain GMX (82230) ☺

G1 Ballistic Coefficient = 0.415

Distance • Yards	Muzzle	100	200	300	400	500	600	800	1000
Velocity • fps	3265	3023	2793	2575	2367	2169	1981	1636	1347
Energy • ft-lbs	3550	3042	2598	2208	1866	1567	1307	892	605
Taylor KO Index	21.5	20.0	18.4	17.0	15.6	14.3	13.1	10.8	8.9
Path • Inches	-1.5	+1.2	0.0	-5.6	-16.5	-33.6	-58.1	-135.6	-265.8
Wind Drift • Inches	0.0	0.6	2.6	6.2	11.4	18.5	27.8	54.2	93.1

Hornady 165-grain SST (82232)

G1 Ballistic Coefficient = 0.447

Distance • Yards	Muzzle	100	200	300	400	500	600	800	1000
Velocity • fps	3185	2964	2753	2552	2360	2176	2000	1677	1399
Energy • ft-lbs	3716	3217	2776	2386	2040	1734	1466	1030	717
Taylor KO Index	23.1	21.5	20.0	18.5	17.1	15.8	14.5	12.2	10.2
Path • Inches	-1.5	+1.2	0.0	-5.8	-17.0	-34.4	-59.2	-136.6	-264.0
Wind Drift • Inches	0.0	0.6	2.5	5.9	10.8	17.5	26.3	50.8	86.7

Hornady 165-grain GMX (82229) ☺

G1 Ballistic Coefficient = 0.447

Distance • Yards	Muzzle	100	200	300	400	500	600	800	1000
Velocity • fps	3130	2911	2703	2504	2314	2132	1959	1640	1369
Energy • ft-lbs	3589	3105	2677	2297	1963	1665	1406	986	686
Taylor KO Index	22.7	21.1	19.6	18.2	16.8	15.5	14.2	11.9	9.9
Path • Inches	-1.5	+1.3	0.0	-6.1	-17.7	-35.8	-61.6	-142.2	-275.1
Wind Drift • Inches	0.0	0.6	2.6	6.0	11.1	18.0	26.9	52.2	89.0

Hornady 180-grain SST (82235)

G1 Ballistic Coefficient = 0.480

Distance • Yards	Muzzle	100	200	300	400	500	600	800	1000
Velocity • fps	3040	2840	2649	2466	2290	2121	1960	1662	1403
Energy • ft-lbs	3693	3223	2804	2430	2096	1799	1536	1104	787
Taylor KO Index	24.1	22.5	21.0	19.5	18.1	16.8	15.5	13.2	11.1
Path • Inches	-1.5	+1.4	0.0	-6.4	-18.5	-37.2	-63.7	-145.4	-278.1
Wind Drift • Inches	0.0	0.6	2.5	5.8	10.6	17.2	25.7	49.6	84.1

.300 Weatherby Magnum

Weatherby 130-grain Barnes TTSX (B300130TTSX) ☺

G1 Ballistic Coefficient = 0.350

Distance • Yards	Muzzle	100	200	300	400	500	600	800	1000
Velocity • fps	3650	3334	3041	2766	2508	2265	2036	1621	1287
Energy • ft-lbs	3847	3209	2670	2210	1817	1481	1196	759	478
Taylor KO Index	20.9	19.1	17.4	15.8	14.3	13.0	11.8	9.3	7.4
Path • Inches	-1.5	+0.8	0.0	-4.6	-13.7	-28.4	-49.9	-120.2	-244.5
Wind Drift • Inches	0.0	0.7	2.8	6.5	12.1	19.8	29.9	59.2	103.6

Weatherby 165 Barnes TSX (B300165TSX) ☺

G1 Ballistic Coefficient = 0.398

Distance • Yards	Muzzle	100	200	300	400	500	600	800	1000
Velocity • fps	3330	3073	2831	2601	2383	2175	1978	1620	1323
Energy • ft-lbs	4064	3460	2936	2479	2080	1734	1434	961	641
Taylor KO Index	24.2	22.3	20.6	18.9	17.3	15.8	14.4	11.8	9.6
Path • Inches	-1.5	+1.1	0.0	-5.4	-16.0	-32.8	-56.9	-133.7	-264.4
Wind Drift • Inches	0.0	0.6	2.7	6.3	11.7	19.0	29.6	55.9	96.6

Weatherby 180 Spitzer (G300180SR)

G1 Ballistic Coefficient = 0.331

Distance • Yards	Muzzle	100	200	300	400	500	600	800	1000
Velocity • fps	3150	2855	2579	2319	2074	1845	1634	1282	1059
Energy • ft-lbs	3967	3259	2659	2150	1720	1361	1068	657	448
Taylor KO Index	24.9	22.6	20.4	18.4	16.4	14.6	12.9	10.2	8.4
Path • Inches	-1.5	+1.4	0.0	-6.6	-19.8	-41.0	-72.5	-178.4	-369.6
Wind Drift • Inches	0.0	0.8	3.6	8.4	15.7	25.9	39.6	79.3	137.2

.300 Remington Ultra Magnum

Remington 165 Copper Solid Tipped (PCS300UMB) ☺

G1 Ballistic Coefficient = 0.447

Distance • Yards	Muzzle	100	200	300	400	500	600	800	1000
Velocity • fps	3260	3035	2821	2617	2422	2235	2057	1727	1440
Energy • ft-lbs	3896	3373	2915	2509	2149	1831	1550	1093	760
Taylor KO Index	23.7	22.0	20.5	19.0	17.6	16.2	14.9	12.5	10.5
Path • Inches	-1.5	+1.1	0.0	-5.5	-16.1	-32.7	-56.2	-129.5	-250.0
Wind Drift • Inches	0.0	0.6	2.4	5.7	10.5	17.0	25.4	49.1	83.7

Remington 180 Swift Scirocco Bonded (PR300UM3)

G1 Ballistic Coefficient = 0.500

Distance • Yards	Muzzle	100	200	300	400	500	600	800	1000
Velocity • fps	3250	3048	2856	2672	2495	2325	2161	1855	1580
Energy • ft-lbs	4221	3714	3260	2853	2487	2160	1868	1376	998
Taylor KO Index	25.7	24.1	22.6	21.2	19.8	18.4	17.1	14.7	12.5
Path • Inches	-1.5	+1.1	0.0	-5.4	-15.7	-31.5	-53.8	-122.0	-231.0
Wind Drift • Inches	0.0	0.5	2.2	5.0	9.2	14.9	22.2	42.5	71.4

Federal 180 Trophy Bonded Tip (P300RUMTT1)

G1 Ballistic Coefficient = 0.498

Distance • Yards	Muzzle	100	200	300	400	500	600	800	1000
Velocity • fps	3200	3000	2810	2630	2450	2280	2119	1815	1544
Energy • ft-lbs	4090	3600	3155	2760	2405	2085	1795	1317	953
Taylor KO Index	25.3	23.8	22.3	20.8	19.4	18.1	16.8	14.4	12.2
Path • Inches	-1.5	+1.2	0.0	-5.6	-16.2	-32.6	-55.8	-126.6	-240.1
Wind Drift • Inches	0.0	0.5	2.2	5.2	9.5	15.3	22.8	43.7	73.8

.30-378 Weatherby Magnum

Weatherby 130-grain Barnes TTSX (B303130TTSX) ☺

G1 Ballistic Coefficient = 0.350

Distance • Yards	Muzzle	100	200	300	400	500	600	800	1000
Velocity • fps	3740	3417	3118	2889	2577	2329	2097	1673	1326
Energy • ft-lbs	4039	3372	2807	2327	1917	1567	1269	808	508
Taylor KO Index	21.4	19.5	17.8	16.2	14.7	13.3	12.0	9.6	7.6
Path • Inches	-1.5	+0.7	0.0	-4.3	-13.0	-26.9	-47.2	-113.6	-230.7
Wind Drift • Inches	0.0	0.6	2.7	6.3	11.7	19.2	28.9	57.1	100.0

Weatherby 165-grain Barnes TSX (B303165TSX) ☺

G1 Ballistic Coefficient = 0.398

Distance • Yards	Muzzle	100	200	300	400	500	600	800	1000
Velocity • fps	3450	3186	2937	2702	2479	2265	2068	1699	1396
Energy • ft-lbs	4362	3719	3161	2675	2251	1882	1567	1057	704
Taylor KO Index	25.0	23.1	21.3	19.6	18.0	16.4	15.0	12.3	10.1
Path • Inches	-1.5	+1.0	0.0	-5.0	-14.8	-30.2	-52.4	-123.0	-242.5
Wind Drift • Inches	0.0	0.6	2.6	6.0	11.1	18.0	27.1	52.9	91.2

Weatherby 180-grain AccuBond (N303180ACB)

1 Ballistic Coefficient = 0.507

Distance • Yards	Muzzle	100	200	300	400	500	600	800	1000
Velocity • fps	3420	3213	3015	2826	2645	2471	2307	1992	1705
Energy • ft-lbs	4676	4126	3634	3193	2797	2441	2127	1586	1163
Taylor KO Index	27.1	25.4	23.9	22.4	20.9	19.6	18.3	15.8	13.5
Path • Inches	-1.5	+0.9	0.0	-4.8	-13.9	-28.0	-47.7	-107.9	-203.5
Wind Drift • Inches	0.0	0.5	2.0	4.7	8.5	13.7	20.4	37.8	65.2

.303 British

Sellier & Bellot 180-grain FMJ (V331302U)

G1 Ballistic Coefficient = 0.505

Distance • Yards	Muzzle	100	200	300	400	500	600	800	1000
Velocity • fps	2438	2272	2112	1959	1813	1674	1545	1318	1146
Energy • ft-lbs	2378	2063	1783	1534	1314	1121	954	695	525
Taylor KO Index	19.5	18.2	16.9	15.7	14.5	13.4	12.4	10.5	9.2
Path • Inches	-1.5	+2.6	0.0	-10.4	-29.9	-60.0	-102.6	-234.0	-445.7
Wind Drift • Inches	0.0	0.8	3.2	7.5	13.9	22.6	33.7	64.5	107.5

.32 Winchester Special

Hornady 165-grain FTX (82732)

G1 Ballistic Coefficient = 0.311

Distance • Yards	Muzzle	100	200	300	400	500	600	800	1000
Velocity • fps	2410	2145	1897	1669	1465	1290	1152	983	882
Energy • ft-lbs	2128	1685	1318	1020	786	610	486	354	285
Taylor KO Index	18.3	16.3	14.4	12.7	11.1	9.8	8.7	7.5	6.7
Path • Inches	-1.5	+3.0	0.0	-12.8	-38.1	-79.6	-142.2	-350.9	-703.4
Wind Drift • Inches	0.0	1.3	5.6	13.4	25.2	41.8	63.3	119.5	189.6

8x57 Mauser JS

Sellier & Bellot 196-grain SPCE (V331812U)

G1 Ballistic Coefficient = 0.286

Distance • Yards	Muzzle	100	200	300	400	500	600	800	1000
Velocity • fps	2591	2292	2012	1755	1523	1324	1167	980	872
Energy • ft-lbs	2932	2286	1763	1341	1010	763	593	418	331
Taylor KO Index	23.4	20.7	18.2	15.9	13.8	12.0	10.6	8.9	7.9
Path • Inches	-1.5	+2.6	0.0	-11.2	-33.8	-71.5	-129.0	-326.3	-668.3
Wind Drift • Inches	0.0	1.3	5.5	13.2	25.2	42.0	64.2	123.2	197.2

.325 Winchester Short Magnum

Winchester 200-grain XP³ (SXP325S)

G1 Ballistic Coefficient = 0.500

Distance • Yards	Muzzle	100	200	300	400	500	600	800	1000
Velocity • fps	2950	2762	2581	2408	2241	2081	1928	1644	1398
Energy • ft-lbs	3864	3387	2959	2574	2230	1923	1651	1201	868
Taylor KO Index	27.8	26.0	24.3	22.9	21.1	19.6	18.2	15.5	13.2
Path • Inches	-1.5	+1.5	0.0	-6.8	-19.5	-39.2	-66.9	-152.1	-289.2
Wind Drift • Inches	0.0	0.6	2.5	5.8	10.6	17.1	25.6	49.2	83.1

.338 RCM (Ruger Compact Magnum)

The .338 RCM is the .338 caliber version of this shortened and nonbelted magnum. The case length is identical with the .308 Winchester, and that allows the .338 RCM to be used in short actions. The performance is, for all practical purposes, identical to the .338 Winchester Magnum.

Hornady 185-grain GMX (82238) ☺

G1 Ballistic Coefficient = 0.420

Distance • Yards	Muzzle	100	200	300	400	500	600	800	1000
Velocity • fps	2980	2755	2542	2338	2143	1958	1784	1471	1223
Energy • ft-lbs	3647	3118	2653	2242	1887	1575	1307	889	615
Taylor KO Index	26.6	24.6	22.7	20.9	19.1	17.5	15.9	13.1	10.9
Path • Inches	-1.5	+1.5	0.0	-6.9	-20.2	-41.2	-71.2	-166.3	-326.5
Wind Drift • Inches	0.0	0.7	2.9	6.9	12.8	20.8	31.4	61.2	104.8

Hornady 200-grain SST (82237)

G1 Ballistic Coefficient = 0.455

Distance • Yards	Muzzle	100	200	300	400	500	600	800	1000
Velocity • fps	2950	2744	2547	2358	2177	2004	1840	1542	1294
Energy • ft-lbs	3846	3342	2879	2468	2104	1784	1504	1056	744
Taylor KO Index	28.5	26.5	24.6	22.8	21.0	19.4	17.8	14.9	12.5
Path • Inches	-1.5	+1.6	0.0	-6.9	-20.1	-40.7	-69.9	-161.2	-311.6
Wind Drift • Inches	0.0	0.7	2.7	6.4	11.8	19.2	28.8	55.7	94.9

Hornady 225-grain SST (82236)

G1 Ballistic Coefficient = 0.515

Distance • Yards	Muzzle	100	200	300	400	500	600	800	1000
Velocity • fps	2750	2575	2407	2245	2089	1940	1798	1537	1316
Energy • ft-lbs	3778	3313	2894	2518	2180	1880	1615	1180	865
Taylor KO Index	29.9	28.0	26.2	24.4	22.7	21.1	19.5	16.7	14.3
Path • Inches	-1.5	+1.9	0.0	-7.9	-22.7	-45.4	-77.5	-175.7	-333.2
Wind Drift • Inches	0.0	0.6	2.6	6.2	11.3	18.4	27.4	52.6	88.6

.338 Winchester Magnum

Hornady 185-grain GMX (82226) ☺

G1 Ballistic Coefficient = 0.420

Distance • Yards	Muzzle	100	200	300	400	500	600	800	1000
Velocity • fps	3080	2850	2632	2424	2226	2036	1857	1533	1270
Energy • ft-lbs	3896	3337	2845	2413	2034	1703	1417	966	662
Taylor KO Index	27.5	25.5	23.5	21.7	19.9	18.2	16.6	13.7	11.3
Path • Inches	-1.5	+1.4	0.0	-6.4	-18.8	-38.2	-66.0	-154.0	-301.9
Wind Drift • Inches	0.0	0.7	2.8	6.6	12.2	19.8	29.8	58.2	99.8

Hornady 200-grain SST (82223)

G1 Ballistic Coefficient = 0.420

Distance • Yards	Muzzle	100	200	300	400	500	600	800	1000
Velocity • fps	3030	2820	2619	2428	2244	2068	1901	1594	1336
Energy • ft-lbs	4076	3531	3047	2617	2236	1899	1605	1129	793
Taylor KO Index	29.3	27.2	25.3	23.4	21.7	20.0	18.4	15.4	12.9
Path • Inches	-1.5	+1.4	0.0	-6.5	-18.9	-38.3	-65.8	-151.5	-292.6
Wind Drift • Inches	0.0	0.6	2.6	6.2	11.4	18.4	27.6	53.5	91.2

Winchester 200-grain E-Tip (S338CT) ☺

G1 Ballistic Coefficient = 0.423

Distance • Yards	Muzzle	100	200	300	400	500	600	800	1000
Velocity • fps	2950	2729	2519	2319	2127	1945	1769	1461	1217
Energy • ft-lbs	3864	3292	2805	2376	1999	1671	1390	948	658
Taylor KO Index	28.5	26.4	24.3	22.4	20.5	18.8	17.1	14.1	11.8
Path • Inches	-1.5	+1.6	0.0	-7.1	-20.6	-41.9	-72.5	-169.4	-332.2
Wind Drift • Inches	0.0	0.7	3.0	6.9	12.8	21.0	31.5	61.5	105.2

Hornady 225-grain SST (82233)

G1 Ballistic Coefficient = 0.515

Distance • Yards	Muzzle	100	200	300	400	500	600	800	1000
Velocity • fps	2840	2662	2490	2325	2166	2014	1868	1599	1367
Energy • ft-lbs	4031	3540	3099	2702	2345	2027	1744	1277	933
Taylor KO Index	30.9	28.9	27.1	25.3	23.5	21.9	20.3	17.4	14.9
Path • Inches	-1.5	+1.7	0.0	-7.3	-21.1	-42.3	-72.0	-163.2	-309.0
Wind Drift • Inches	0.0	0.6	2.5	5.9	10.8	17.5	26.1	50.1	84.5

.338 Lapua Magnum

Nosler 225-grain AccuBond (28039)

G1 Ballistic Coefficient = 0.549

Distance • Yards	Muzzle	100	200	300	400	500	600	800	1000
Velocity • fps	3025	2850	2682	2521	2365	2214	2069	1796	1551
Energy • ft-lbs	4571	4058	3594	3175	2798	2449	2139	1613	1202
Taylor KO Index	32.9	31.0	29.1	27.4	25.7	24.1	22.5	19.5	16.9
Path • Inches	-1.5	+1.4	0.0	-6.2	-17.9	-35.9	-60.9	-136.6	-255.7
Wind Drift • Inches	0.0	0.5	2.2	5.0	9.2	14.8	22.0	41.9	70.8

Nosler 250-grain AccuBond (28075)

G1 Ballistic Coefficient = 0.584

Distance • Yards	Muzzle	100	200	300	400	500	600	800	1000
Velocity • fps	2850	2692	2539	2392	2250	2112	1979	1729	1505
Energy • ft-lbs	4508	4022	3578	3176	2810	2476	2174	1660	1258
Taylor KO Index	34.4	32.5	30.6	28.9	27.2	25.5	23.9	20.9	18.2
Path • Inches	-1.5	+1.6	0.0	-7.0	-20.2	-40.2	-68.0	-151.6	-282.0
Wind Drift • Inches	0.0	0.5	2.2	5.1	9.3	15.0	22.4	42.0	70.9

Lapua 300-grain Scenar (4318013)

G1 Ballistic Coefficient = 0.739

Distance • Yards	Muzzle	100	200	300	400	500	600	800	1000
Velocity • fps	2723	2600	2482	2367	2255	2145	2042	1842	1653
Energy • ft-lbs	4938	4504	4102	3731	3387	3066	2778	2259	1819
Taylor KO Index	39.4	37.7	36.0	34.3	32.7	31.1	29.6	26.7	23.9
Path • Inches	-1.5	+1.8	0.0	-7.5	-21.1	-41.6	-106.2	-151.9	-275.5
Wind Drift • Inches	0.0	0.4	1.8	4.2	7.7	12.3	18.2	34.0	55.9

9.3x74R

Nosler 250-grain AccuBond (33033)

G1 Ballistic Coefficient = 0.495

Distance • Yards	Muzzle	100	200	300	400	500	600	800	1000
Velocity • fps	2550	2375	2208	2048	1895	1749	1613	1370	1179
Energy • ft-lbs	3609	3132	2706	2328	1993	1698	1444	1042	772
Taylor KO Index	33.5	31.2	29.0	26.9	24.9	23.0	21.2	18.0	15.5
Path • Inches	-1.5	+2.3	0.0	-9.5	-27.2	-54.7	-93.6	-213.8	-408.7
Wind Drift • Inches	0.0	0.7	3.1	7.2	13.3	21.6	32.3	62.1	104.0

Federal 286-grain Swift A-Frame (P93745A)

G1 Ballistic Coefficient = 0.384

Distance • Yards	Muzzle	100	200	300	400	500	600	800	1000
Velocity • fps	2360	2150	1950	1760	1580	1420	1283	1083	966
Energy • ft-lbs	3535	2930	2405	1960	1590	1285	1046	745	593
Taylor KO Index	35.5	32.3	29.3	26.5	23.8	21.4	19.3	16.3	14.5
Path • Inches	-1.5	+3.0	0.0	-12.3	-35.8	-73.4	-128.2	-305.6	-601.2
Wind Drift • Inches	0.0	1.1	4.6	10.8	20.1	33.0	49.8	95.2	154.2

Nosler 250-grain Partition (33048)

G1 Ballistic Coefficient = 0.483

Distance • Yards	Muzzle	100	200	300	400	500	600	800	1000
Velocity • fps	2300	2132	1971	1818	1673	1538	1414	1208	1067
Energy • ft-lbs	3359	2886	2467	2099	1777	1502	1271	927	723
Taylor KO Index	34.6	32.1	29.6	27.3	25.2	23.1	21.3	18.2	16.0
Path • Inches	-1.5	+3.1	0.0	-12.0	-34.6	-69.7	-119.4	-274.2	-524.5
Wind Drift • Inches	0.0	0.9	3.7	8.6	16.0	25.9	38.8	73.9	121.4

Hornady 286-grain SP-RP (82304)

G1 Ballistic Coefficient = 0.365

Distance • Yards	Muzzle	100	200	300	400	500	600	800	1000
Velocity • fps	2360	2136	1924	1727	1545	1383	1245	1053	943
Energy • ft-lbs	3536	2896	2351	1893	1516	1214	965	705	565
Taylor KO Index	35.7	32.3	29.1	26.1	23.4	20.9	18.8	15.9	14.3
Path • Inches	-1.5	+3.1	0.0	-12.5	-36.7	75.5	-132.6	-318.5	-629.5
Wind Drift • Inches	0.0	1.2	4.8	11.4	21.4	35.2	53.1	101.2	162.9

Federal 286-grain Barnes Triple-Shock X-Bullet (P9374C) ☺

G1 Ballistic Coefficient = 0.411

Distance • Yards	Muzzle	100	200	300	400	500	600	800	1000
Velocity • fps	2360	2160	1970	1770	1630	1470	1335	1125	990
Energy • ft-lbs	3535	2965	2465	2035	1675	1375	1132	804	634
Taylor KO Index	35.7	32.7	29.8	27.1	24.6	22.2	20.2	17.0	15.1
Path • Inches	-1.5	+3.0	0.0	-12.0	-34.8	-70.8	-123.0	-289.8	-566.2
Wind Drift • Inches	0.0	1.0	4.2	10.0	18.6	30.4	45.7	87.6	142.9

Federal 286-grain Barnes Banded Solid (P9374D) ☺

G1 Ballistic Coefficient = 0.259

Distance • Yards	Muzzle	100	200	300	400	500	600	800	1000
Velocity • fps	2360	2050	1760	1500	1290	1130	1023	890	798
Energy • ft-lbs	3535	2660	1965	1435	1055	805	665	505	405
Taylor KO Index	35.5	30.8	26.5	22.6	19.4	17.0	15.4	13.4	12.0
Path • Inches	-1.5	+3.4	0.0	-14.7	-44.9	-96.0	-174.2	-435.6	-872.8
Wind Drift • Inches	0.0	1.6	7.1	17.2	32.7	54.2	81.0	147.6	228.6

.375 Holland & Holland Magnum

Winchester 300-grain Nosler Partition (S375SLSP)

G1 Ballistic Coefficient = 0.398

Distance • Yards	Muzzle	100	200	300	400	500	600	800	1000
Velocity • fps	2530	2376	2112	1919	1737	1569	1417	1174	1024
Energy • ft-lbs	4263	3572	2970	2452	2010	1640	1338	919	699
Taylor KO Index	40.8	37.3	34.0	30.9	28.0	25.3	22.8	18.9	16.5
Path • Inches	-1.5	+2.5	0.0	-10.3	-30.1	-61.5	-107.0	-253.8	-501.5
Wind Drift • Inches	0.0	1.0	4.0	9.3	17.4	28.5	43.0	83.6	138.7

Federal 300-grain Swift A-Frame (P375SA)

G1 Ballistic Coefficient = 0.325

Distance • Yards	Muzzle	100	200	300	400	500	600	800	1000
Velocity • fps	2450	2190	1950	1730	1530	1350	1203	1015	907
Energy • ft-lbs	4000	3205	2540	1995	1555	1215	964	686	549
Taylor KO Index	39.5	35.3	31.4	27.9	24.7	21.8	19.4	16.4	14.3
Path • Inches	-1.5	+2.9	0.0	-12.0	-35.8	-74.4	-132.3	-325.1	-652.7
Wind Drift • Inches	0.0	1.2	5.2	12.4	23.3	38.6	58.6	111.9	179.3

Winchester 300-grain Nosler Solid (S375SLS) ☺

G1 Ballistic Coefficient = 0.198

Distance • Yards	Muzzle	100	200	300	400	500	600	800	1000
Velocity • fps	2530	2110	1734	1413	1170	1021	928	799	703
Energy • ft-lbs	4263	2965	2002	1329	911	694	573	426	329
Taylor KO Index	40.8	34.0	27.9	22.8	18.9	16.5	15.0	12.9	11.3
Path • Inches	-1.5	+3.2	0.0	-15.0	-47.5	-105.4	-196.6	-507.2	-1037
Wind Drift • Inches	0.0	2.0	8.7	21.7	42.0	69.8	103.3	184.8	284.6

.375 Weatherby Magnum

Nosler 260-grain AccuBond (36008)

G1 Ballistic Coefficient = 0.473

Distance • Yards	Muzzle	100	200	300	400	500	600	800	1000
Velocity • fps	3000	2799	2606	2422	2245	2076	1915	1618	1364
Energy • ft-lbs	5195	4521	3921	3386	2910	2489	2118	1512	1074
Taylor KO Index	41.9	39.1	36.4	33.8	31.4	29.0	26.7	22.6	19.0
Path • Inches	-1.5	+1.5	0.0	-6.6	-19.1	-38.6	-66.1	-151.3	-290.2
Wind Drift • Inches	0.0	0.6	2.6	6.0	11.0	17.9	26.7	51.6	87.6

.444 Marlin

Hornady 265-grain FTX (82744)

G1 Ballistic Coefficient = 0.225

Distance • Yards	Muzzle	100	200	300	400	500	600	800	1000
Velocity • fps	2325	1971	1652	1380	1171	1035	948	827	736
Energy • ft-lbs	3180	2285	1606	1120	807	631	529	402	319
Taylor KO Index	37.8	32.1	26.9	22.5	19.1	16.8	15.4	13.5	12.0
Path • Inches	-1.5	+3.8	0.0	-16.6	-51.7	-112.0	-204.8	-512.5	-1025
Wind Drift • Inches	0.0	2.0	8.5	20.8	39.8	65.3	90.6	170.4	261.0

.45-70 Government

Hornady 325-grain FTX (13063)

G1 Ballistic Coefficient = 0.230

Distance • Yards	Muzzle	100	200	300	400	500	600	800	1000
Velocity • fps	2050	1729	1450	1225	1072	974	847	798	714
Energy • ft-lbs	3032	2158	1516	1083	829	685	590	459	368
Taylor KO Index	43.6	36.8	30.8	26.0	22.8	20.7	18.0	17.0	15.2
Path • Inches	-1.5	+5.1	0.0	-21.8	-66.9	-142.0	-253.8	-611.2	-1188
Wind Drift • Inches	0.0	2.3	9.9	23.9	44.4	70.5	101.1	174.4	263.5

Winchester 375-grain Dual Bond (S4570B)

G1 Ballistic Coefficient = 0.267

Distance • Yards	Muzzle	100	200	300	400	500	600	800	1000
Velocity • fps	1500	1292	1135	1029	955	897	848	767	699
Energy • ft-lbs	1873	1391	1072	881	759	670	599	490	406
Taylor KO Index	36.8	31.7	27.8	25.2	23.4	22.8	20.8	18.8	17.2
Path • Inches	-1.5	+9.7	0.0	-36.6	-106.1	-213.7	-364.5	-816.9	-1508
Wind Drift • Inches	0.0	2.8	11.3	25.1	43.3	65.3	90.7	151.7	226.4

.50 BMG (Browning Machine Gun)

The .50 BMG's history dates from about the beginning of WWI. It was, as the name implies, designed for John Browning's heavy machine gun. In addition to its use as a mount on a tripod, the gun found applications on ground vehicles. During most of WWII, it was the primary aircraft machine gun. Sometime in the 1980s a group of shooters formed the .50 Caliber Shooters Association to use guns in .50 BMG caliber for long-range competition. Unfortunately, the surplus military ammunition is not nearly accurate enough for this purpose, and various companies have, from time to time, manufactured high-quality target ammo in this caliber.

Hornady 750-grain A-MAX (8270)

G1 Ballistic Coefficient = 0.500

Distance • Yards	Muzzle	100	200	300	400	500	600	800	1000
Velocity • fps	2815	2632	2457	2288	2126	1971	1823	1552	1322
Energy • ft-lbs	13197	11538	10052	8719	7528	6468	5536	4011	2910
Taylor KO Index	153.2	143.3	133.7	124.5	115.7	107.3	99.2	84.5	72.0
Path • Inches	-1.5	+1.8	0.0	-7.5	-21.7	-43.6	-74.4	-169.4	-322.6
Wind Drift • Inches	0.0	0.6	2.6	6.2	11.3	18.4	27.5	52.8	89.2

Data for Calibers Suitable for Dangerous Game

.450-400 Nitro Express 3"

Hornady has opted to support this classic caliber. British convention in naming cartridges that are formed by necking down (or up) another cartridge is to put the parent cartridge first and the "necked-to" size second. So the .450-400 is a .450 Nitro Express necked to .400 caliber. That's exactly the opposite of the convention in the U.S.A. This is an oldie and has been largely made obsolete by the .375 H&H.

Hornady 400-grain DGX (82433)

G1 Ballistic Coefficient = 0.326

Distance • Yards	Muzzle	50	100	150	200	250	300	400	500
Velocity • fps	2050	1933	1820	1712	1608	1512	1420	1260	1135
Energy • ft-lbs	3732	3319	2941	2604	2298	2030	1791	1412	1145
Taylor KO Index	47.8	45.1	42.4	39.9	37.5	35.3	31.3	29.4	26.5
Path • Inches	-0.9	+1.8	+2.2	0.0	-5.2	-13.8	-26.1	-64.3	-124.4
Wind Drift • Inches	0.0	0.4	1.6	3.7	6.7	10.8	15.9	29.6	48.1

Hornady 400-grain DGS (8242)

G1 Ballistic Coefficient = 0.326

Distance • Yards	Muzzle	50	100	150	200	250	300	400	500
Velocity • fps	2050	1933	1820	1712	1608	1512	1420	1260	1135
Energy • ft-lbs	3732	3319	2941	2604	2298	2030	1791	1412	1145
Taylor KO Index	47.8	45.1	42.4	39.9	37.5	35.3	31.3	29.4	26.5
Path • Inches	-0.9	+1.8	+2.2	0.0	-5.2	-13.8	-26.1	-64.3	-124.4
Wind Drift • Inches	0.0	0.4	1.6	3.7	6.7	10.8	15.9	29.6	48.1

.404 Jeffery

Hornady 400-grain DGX (8239)

G1 Ballistic Coefficient = 0.315

Distance • Yards	Muzzle	50	100	150	200	250	300	400	500
Velocity • fps	2300	2170	2046	1924	1809	1697	1592	1399	1238
Energy • ft-lbs	4698	4185	3716	3289	2906	2557	2251	1738	1362
Taylor KO Index	53.9	50.8	47.9	45.1	42.4	39.8	37.3	32.8	29.0
Path • Inches	-0.9	+1.3	+1.7	0.0	-4.0	-10.8	-20.5	-50.8	-98.9
Wind Drift • Inches	0.0	0.3	1.4	3.2	5.9	9.5	14.1	26.6	43.8

Hornady 400-grain DGS (8238)

G1 Ballistic Coefficient = 0.315

Distance • Yards	Muzzle	50	100	150	200	250	300	400	500
Velocity • fps	2300	2170	2046	1924	1809	1697	1592	1399	1238
Energy • ft-lbs	4698	4185	3716	3289	2906	2557	2251	1738	1362
Taylor KO Index	53.9	50.8	47.9	45.1	42.4	39.8	37.3	32.8	29.0
Path • Inches	-0.9	+1.3	+1.7	0.0	-4.0	-10.8	-20.5	-50.8	-98.9
Wind Drift • Inches	0.0	0.3	1.4	3.2	5.9	9.5	14.1	26.6	43.8

.416 Rigby

Hornady 400-grain DGX (82663)

G1 Ballistic Coefficient = 0.320

Distance • Yards	Muzzle	50	100	150	200	250	300	400	500
Velocity • fps	2415	2284	2157	2034	1915	1801	1691	1490	1316
Energy • ft-lbs	5180	4634	4131	3675	3256	2882	2540	1973	1538
Taylor KO Index	57.4	54.3	51.3	48.4	45.5	42.8	40.2	35.4	31.3
Path • Inches	-0.9	+1.1	+1.5	0.0	-3.6	-9.6	-18.2	-45.1	-87.7
Wind Drift • Inches	0.0	0.3	1.3	2.9	5.4	8.7	12.9	24.3	40.2

Hornady 400-grain DGS (8265)

G1 Ballistic Coefficient = 0.320

Distance • Yards	Muzzle	50	100	150	200	250	300	400	500
Velocity • fps	2415	2284	2157	2034	1915	1801	1691	1490	1316
Energy • ft-lbs	5180	4634	4131	3675	3256	2882	2540	1973	1538
Taylor KO Index	57.4	54.3	51.3	48.4	45.5	42.8	40.2	35.4	31.3
Path • Inches	-0.9	+1.1	+1.5	0.0	-3.6	-9.6	-18.2	-45.1	-87.7
Wind Drift • Inches	0.0	0.3	1.3	2.9	5.4	8.7	12.9	24.3	40.2

Federal 400-grain Swift A-Frame (P416SA)

G1 Ballistic Coefficient = 0.366

Distance • Yards	Muzzle	50	100	150	200	250	300	400	500
Velocity • fps	2350	2237	2130	2020	1920	1816	1720	1540	1380
Energy • ft-lbs	4905	4446	4020	3625	3265	2931	2635	2110	1695
Taylor KO Index	55.9	53.2	50.6	48.0	45.6	43.2	40.9	36.6	32.8
Path • Inches	-0.9	+1.2	+1.6	0.0	-3.7	-9.8	-18.4	-30.1	-86.3
Wind Drift • Inches	0.0	0.3	1.2	2.6	4.8	7.8	11.5	21.4	35.2

Federal 400-grain Barnes Banded Solid (P416E)

G1 Ballistic Coefficient = 0.320

Distance • Yards	Muzzle	50	100	150	200	250	300	400	500
Velocity • fps	2400	2293	2190	2090	1990	1890	1800	1630	1460
Energy • ft-lbs	4700	4669	4255	3865	3515	3174	2875	2345	1905
Taylor KO Index	57.1	54.5	52.1	49.7	47.3	44.9	42.8	38.7	34.7
Path • Inches	-0.9	+1.1	+1.5	0.0	-3.5	-9.1	-17.2	-41.8	-79.6
Wind Drift • Inches	0.0	0.2	1.0	2.4	4.4	7.0	10.3	19.3	31.6

.416 Remington Magnum

Federal 400-grain Swift A-Frame (P416RSA)

G1 Ballistic Coefficient = 0.365

Distance • Yards	Muzzle	50	100	150	200	250	300	400	500
Velocity • fps	2400	2285	2180	2065	1960	1858	1760	1580	1410
Energy • ft-lbs	5115	4640	4200	3789	3420	3087	2760	2153	1775
Taylor KO Index	57.1	54.3	51.8	49.1	46.6	44.2	41.8	37.6	33.5
Path • Inches	-0.9	+1.1	+1.5	0.0	-3.5	-9.3	-17.6	-43.0	-82.4
Wind Drift • Inches	0.0	0.3	1.1	2.6	4.7	7.5	11.1	20.9	34.3

Federal 400-grain Barnes Banded Solid (P416RB)

G1 Ballistic Coefficient = 0.390

Distance • Yards	Muzzle	50	100	150	200	250	300	400	500
Velocity • fps	2400	2293	2190	2086	1990	1890	1790	1620	1460
Energy • ft-lbs	5115	4669	4250	3865	3500	3174	2860	2325	1885
Taylor KO Index	57.1	54.5	52.1	49.6	47.3	44.9	42.6	38.5	37.4
Path • Inches	-0.9	+1.1	+1.5	0.0	-3.5	-9.1	-17.2	-41.8	-79.6
Wind Drift • Inches	0.0	0.3	1.0	2.4	4.4	7.0	10.3	19.3	31.6

.416 Ruger

The world needs another .416 cartridge like [it needs] the return of the plague. The .416 Ruger is a nonbelted magnum with a cartridge case length of 2.580 inches. That's only very slightly longer than the .458 Winchester cartridge, and, therefore, this cartridge will undoubtedly fit into standard length actions. The performance is in the same ballpark as the .416 Remington Magnum. Hornady worked with Ruger to develop this cartridge.

Hornady 400-grain DGX (82665)

G1 Ballistic Coefficient = 0.330

Distance • Yards	Muzzle	50	100	150	200	250	300	400	500
Velocity • fps	2400	2273	2151	2031	1917	1805	1700	1502	1331
Energy • ft-lbs	5116	4591	4109	3666	3264	2896	2568	2006	1573
Taylor KO Index	57.1	54.0	51.1	48.3	45.6	42.9	40.6	35.7	31.6
Path • Inches	-1.5	+1.2	+1.5	0.0	-3.6	-9.6	-18.3	-45.0	-87.2
Wind Drift • Inches	0.0	0.3	1.2	2.9	5.3	8.4	12.5	23.6	39.0

Hornady 400-grain DGS (82666)

G1 Ballistic Coefficient = 0.330

Distance • Yards	Muzzle	50	100	150	200	250	300	400	500
Velocity • fps	2400	2273	2151	2031	1917	1805	1700	1502	1331
Energy • ft-lbs	5116	4591	4109	3666	3264	2896	2568	2006	1573
Taylor KO Index	57.1	54.0	51.1	48.3	45.6	42.9	40.6	35.7	31.6
Path • Inches	-1.5	+1.2	+1.5	0.0	-3.6	-9.6	-18.3	-45.0	-87.2
Wind Drift • Inches	0.0	0.3	1.2	2.9	5.3	8.4	12.5	23.6	39.0

.450 Nitro Express 3¼ Inch

Hornady 480-grain DGX (8255)

G1 Ballistic Coefficient = 0.276

Distance • Yards	Muzzle	50	100	150	200	250	300	400	500
Velocity • fps	2150	2008	1872	1742	1618	1504	1397	1218	1087
Energy • ft-lbs	4927	4299	3733	3235	2792	2412	2080	1580	1260
Taylor KO Index	67.5	63.1	58.8	54.7	50.8	47.2	43.9	38.3	34.1
Path • Inches	-0.9	+1.7	+2.1	0.0	-4.9	-13.2	-25.3	-63.6	-125.3
Wind Drift • Inches	0.0	0.4	1.8	4.1	7.6	12.2	18.1	34.1	55.6

Hornady 480-grain DGS (8256)

G1 Ballistic Coefficient = 0.276

Distance • Yards	Muzzle	50	100	150	200	250	300	400	500
Velocity • fps	2150	2008	1872	1742	1618	1504	1397	1218	1087
Energy • ft-lbs	4927	4299	3733	3235	2792	2412	2080	1580	1260
Taylor KO Index	67.5	63.1	58.8	54.7	50.8	47.2	43.9	38.3	34.1
Path • Inches	-0.9	+1.7	+2.1	0.0	-4.9	-13.2	-25.3	-63.6	-125.3
Wind Drift • Inches	0.0	0.4	1.8	4.1	7.6	12.2	18.1	34.1	55.6

.458 Winchester Magnum

Federal 500-grain Swift A-Frame (P458SA)

G1 Ballistic Coefficient = 0.360

Distance • Yards	Muzzle	50	100	150	200	250	300	400	500
Velocity • fps	2090	1983	1880	1778	1680	1590	1500	1350	1210
Energy • ft-lbs	4850	4365	3915	3511	3145	2806	2510	2010	1630
Taylor KO Index	68.4	64.9	61.5	58.2	55.0	52.0	49.1	44.2	39.6
Path • Inches	-0.9	+1.7	+2.1	0.0	-4.8	-12.7	-24.1	-58.8	-112.8
Wind Drift • Inches	0.0	0.3	1.4	3.2	5.8	9.4	13.8	25.8	41.9

Federal 500-grain Trophy Bonded Bear Claw (P458T2)

G1 Ballistic Coefficient = 0.284

Distance • Yards	Muzzle	50	100	150	200	250	300	400	500
Velocity • fps	2090	1954	1820	1700	1580	1474	1370	1200	1080
Energy • ft-lbs	4850	4241	3685	3211	2775	2412	2080	1595	1285
Taylor KO Index	68.4	63.9	59.5	55.6	49.1	48.2	44.8	39.3	35.3
Path • Inches	-0.9	+1.8	+2.2	0.0	-5.2	-13.9	-26.6	-66.5	-130.4
Wind Drift • Inches	0.0	0.4	1.8	4.1	7.6	12.3	18.2	34.1	55.3

Winchester 500-grain Nosler Partition (S458WSLSP

G1 Ballistic Coefficient = 0.330

Distance • Yards	Muzzle	50	100	150	200	250	300	400	500
Velocity • fps	2010	1896	1786	1680	1580	1486	1397	1243	1124
Energy • ft-lbs	4485	3991	3538	3135	2771	2451	2168	1715	1401
Taylor KO Index	65.8	62.0	58.4	55.0	51.7	48.6	45.7	40.7	36.8
Path • Inches	-0.9	+1.9	+2.3	0.0	-5.4	-14.3	-27.1	-66.7	-128.8
Wind Drift • Inches	0.0	0.4	1.6	3.7	6.8	10.9	16.1	29.9	48.1

Hornady 500-grain DGX Superformance (85833)

G1 Ballistic Coefficient = 0.360

Distance • Yards	Muzzle	50	100	150	200	250	300	400	500
Velocity • fps	2140	2007	1880	1758	1643	1532	1432	1254	1119
Energy • ft-lbs	5084	4475	3926	3422	2996	2608	2276	1745	1392
Taylor KO Index	70.0	65.7	61.5	57.5	53.7	50.1	46.8	41.0	36.6
Path • Inches	-0.9	+1.7	+2.1	0.0	-4.9	-13.0	-24.8	-61.8	-120.9
Wind Drift • Inches	0.0	0.4	1.7	3.8	7.0	11.4	16.9	31.7	51.7

Hornady 500-grain DGS (8585)

G1 Ballistic Coefficient = 0.360

Distance • Yards	Muzzle	50	100	150	200	250	300	400	500
Velocity • fps	2140	2007	1880	1758	1643	1532	1432	1254	1119
Energy • ft-lbs	5084	4475	3926	3422	2996	2608	2276	1745	1392
Taylor KO Index	70.0	65.7	61.5	57.5	53.7	50.1	46.8	41.0	36.6
Path • Inches	-0.9	+1.7	+2.1	0.0	-4.9	-13.0	-24.8	-61.8	-120.9
Wind Drift • Inches	0.0	0.4	1.7	3.8	7.0	11.4	16.9	31.7	51.7

Federal 500-grain Barnes Banded Solid (P458E) ☺

G1 Ballistic Coefficient = 0.393

Distance • Yards	Muzzle	50	100	150	200	250	300	400	500
Velocity • fps	2050	1953	1860	1767	1680	1594	1520	1370	1240
Energy • ft-lbs	4665	4234	3830	3466	3130	2822	2545	2075	1710
Taylor KO Index	67.1	63.9	60.8	57.8	55.0	52.1	49.7	44.8	40.6
Path • Inches	-0.9	+1.8	+2.1	0.0	-4.9	-12.9	-24.4	-59.0	-112.4
Wind Drift • Inches	0.0	0.3	1.3	3.0	5.4	8.7	12.8	17.8	38.7

Winchester 500-grain Nosler Solid (S458WSLS) ☺

G1 Ballistic Coefficient = 0.243

Distance • Yards	Muzzle	50	100	150	200	250	300	400	500
Velocity • fps	2010	1856	1710	1573	1447	1333	1233	1083	986
Energy • ft-lbs	4485	3824	3246	2747	2323	1973	1688	1302	1080
Taylor KO Index	65.8	60.7	55.9	51.5	47.3	43.6	40.3	35.4	32.3
Path • Inches	-0.9	+2.0	+2.5	0.0	-6.0	-16.3	-31.4	-79.6	-157.3
Wind Drift • Inches	0.0	0.5	2.2	5.2	9.6	15.4	22.9	42.5	67.5

.470 Nitro Express

Federal 500-grain Barnes Triple-Shock X-Bullet (P470C) ☺

G1 Ballistic Coefficient = 0.363

Distance • Yards	Muzzle	50	100	150	200	250	300	400	500
Velocity • fps	2150	2042	1940	1835	1740	1643	1550	1390	1250
Energy • ft-lbs	5130	4629	4160	3739	3350	2998	2680	2140	1730
Taylor KO Index	72.8	69.1	65.7	62.1	58.9	55.6	52.5	47.1	42.3
Path • Inches	-0.9	+1.6	+1.9	0.0	-4.5	-11.9	-22.6	-55.1	-105.6
Wind Drift • Inches	0.0	0.3	1.3	3.0	5.6	8.9	13.2	24.6	40.1

Federal 500-grain Swift A-Frame (P470SA)

G1 Ballistic Coefficient = 0.363

Distance • Yards	Muzzle	50	100	150	200	250	300	400	500
Velocity • fps	2150	2042	1940	1835	1740	1643	1550	1390	1250
Energy • ft-lbs	5130	4629	4160	3739	3350	2998	2680	2140	1730
Taylor KO Index	72.8	69.1	65.7	62.1	58.9	55.6	52.5	47.1	42.3
Path • Inches	-0.9	+1.6	+1.9	0.0	-4.5	-11.9	-22.6	-55.1	-105.6
Wind Drift • Inches	0.0	0.3	1.3	3.0	5.6	8.9	13.2	24.6	40.1

Federal 500-grain Barnes Banded Solid (P470D) ☺

G1 Ballistic Coefficient = 0.241

Distance • Yards	Muzzle	50	100	150	200	250	300	400	500
Velocity • fps	2150	1988	1840	1688	1560	1426	1320	1140	1020
Energy • ft-lbs	5130	4389	3740	3136	2690	2260	1930	1440	1165
Taylor KO Index	72.8	67.3	62.3	57.2	52.8	48.3	44.7	38.6	34.5
Path • Inches	-0.9	+1.7	+2.2	0.0	-5.2	-14.1	-27.2	-69.4	-138.5
Wind Drift • Inches	0.0	0.5	2.0	4.8	8.8	14.3	21.3	40.2	64.8

.17 Remington Fireball

When Remington introduced its XP-100 Pistol in 1964, the company also introduced a new cartridge designed especially for the XP-100. The .221 Remington Fireball was a shortened .222 Remington with a little less performance. Shooters grabbed the XP-100 and rebarreled it in numerous calibers, anything but the .221. Remington finally stopped making the .221 but recently restarted production; it also introduced this .17 Remington Fireball cartridge.

Relative Recoil Factor = 0.43

Specifications:

Controlling Agency for Standardization of this Ammunition: SAAMI

Bullet Weight	Velocity	Maximum Average Pressure	
Grains	fps	Copper Crusher	Transducer
xx	xxxx	52,000 cup	N/S

Standard barrel for velocity testing: 10.50 inches long • 1 turn in 12 inch twist

Availability:

Remington 20-grain Accutip-V (PRA17FB

G1 Ballistic Coefficient = 0.185

Distance • Yards	Muzzle	100	200	300	400	500	600	800	1000
Velocity • fps	4000	3380	2840	2360	1930	1555	1255	949	806
Energy • ft-lbs	710	507	358	247	165	107	70	40	29
Taylor KO Index	2.0	1.7	1.4	1.2	1.0	0.8	0.6	0.5	0.4
Path • Inches	-1.5	+0.8	0.0	-5.2	-16.6	-37.6	-73.2	-219.4	-519.7
Wind Drift • Inches	0.0	1.2	5.0	12.2	23.7	41.1	65.8	138.9	233.4

Remington 25-grain UMC Jacketed Hollow Point (L17FBV)

G1 Ballistic Coefficient = 0.193

Distance • Yards	Muzzle	100	200	300	400	500	600	800	1000
Velocity • fps	3850	3280	2780	2330	1925	1569	1276	966	823
Energy • ft-lbs	823	597	429	301	206	137	90	52	38
Taylor KO Index	2.4	2.1	1.8	1.5	1.2	1.0	0.8	0.6	0.5
Path • Inches	-1.5	+0.9	0.0	-5.4	-17.4	-38.9	-74.8	-219.3	-512.3
Wind Drift • Inches	0.0	1.2	5.0	12.0	23.3	40.0	63.8	133.6	225.3

.32 Smith & Wesson Long

Magtech 98-grain LWC (32SWLB)

G1 Ballistic Coefficient = 0.030

Distance • Yards	Muzzle	25	50	75	100	125	150	175	200
Velocity • fps	682	615	554	499	449	402	360	322	288
Energy • ft-lbs	101	82	67	54	44	36	29	23	18
Taylor KO Index	3.0	2.7	2.4	2.2	2.0	1.8	1.6	1.4	1.3
Mid-Range Trajectory Height • Inches	0.0	0.3	2.6	6.8	14.0	24.7	40.3	63.1	92.9
Drop • Inches	0.0	-2.5	-10.8	-26.2	-50.3	-85.3	-133.8	-199.1	-285.6

Magtech 98-grain SJHP (32SWLC)

G1 Ballistic Coefficient = 0.013

Distance • Yards	Muzzle	25	50	75	100	125	150	175	200
Velocity • fps	778	610	479	373	287	219	166	127	66
Energy • ft-lbs	132	81	50	30	18	10	6.0	3.5	0.9
Taylor KO Index	3.4	2.7	2.1	1.6	1.3	1.0	0.7	0.5	0.3
Mid-Range Trajectory Height • Inches	0.0	1.8	3.0	8.5	18.5	36.1	65.1	112.2	183.3
Drop • Inches	0.0	-2.1	-10.2	-28.0	-61.8	-111.0	-196.6	-303.5	-492.4

Sellier & Bellot 100-grain WC (V311302U)

G1 Ballistic Coefficient = 0.074

Distance • Yards	Muzzle	25	50	75	100	125	150	175	200
Velocity • fps	735	704	675	647	620	595	570	547	524
Energy • ft-lbs	120	110	101	93	85	79	72	66	61
Taylor KO Index	3.3	3.2	3.0	2.9	2.8	2.7	2.6	2.5	2.4
Mid-Range Trajectory Height • Inches	0.0	0.2	1.8	4.7	9.1	15.0	23.0	32.8	45.1
Drop • Inches	0.0	-2.1	-8.5	-19.8	-36.2	-58.2	-86.4	-121.4	-163.5

Fiocchi 100-grain LWC (32LA)

G1 Ballistic Coefficient = 0.028

Distance • Yards	Muzzle	25	50	75	100	125	150	175	200
Velocity • fps	730	652	583	522	466	415	368	327	289
Energy • ft-lbs	116	95	74	60	47	38	30	24	19
Taylor KO Index	3.3	2.9	2.6	2.3	2.1	1.9	1.7	1.5	1.3
Mid-Range Trajectory Height • Inches	0.0	0.2	2.2	6.1	12.5	22.5	37.0	58.6	87.2
Drop • Inches	0.0	-2.2	-9.5	-23.3	-45.0	-76.8	-121.3	-181.9	-263.0

.32 Auto (7.65mm Browning)

Cor-Bon 55-grain Pow'RBall (PB3255/20)

G1 Ballistic Coefficient = 0.100

Distance • Yards	Muzzle	25	50	75	100	125	150	175	200
Velocity • fps	1100	1033	980	936	899	865	834	806	779
Energy • ft-lbs	148	130	117	107	99	91	85	79	74
Taylor KO Index	2.7	2.5	2.4	2.3	2.2	2.1	2.0	2.0	1.9
Mid-Range Trajectory Height • Inches	0.0	0.2	1.0	2.4	4.5	7.4	11.2	15.7	21.5
Drop • Inches	0.0	-0.9	-3.9	-9.2	-16.8	-27.2	-40.6	-57.0	-76.7

Magtech 65-grain JHP (GG32A)

G1 Ballistic Coefficient = 0.149

Distance • Yards	Muzzle	25	50	75	100	125	150	175	200
Velocity • fps	922	897	874	853	833	813	795	777	761
Energy • ft-lbs	123	116	110	105	100	96	91	87	84
Taylor KO Index	2.7	2.6	2.5	2.5	2.4	2.4	2.3	2.3	2.2
Mid-Range Trajectory Height • Inches	0.0	0.1	0.8	2.7	5.3	8.5	13.0	18.2	24.7
Drop • Inches	0.0	-1.3	-5.3	-12.1	-22.0	-34.9	-51.2	-70.8	-94.1

.327 Federal Magnum

American Eagle (Federal) 85-grain (AE327A)

G1 Ballistic Coefficient = 0.140

Distance • Yards	Muzzle	25	50	75	100	125	150	175	200
Velocity • fps	1400	1310	1220	1150	1090	1043	1003	968	938
Energy • ft-lbs	588	511	447	396	357	326	301	281	264
Taylor KO Index	5.6	8.4	7.9	7.3	6.9	6.6	6.3	6.0	5.8
Mid-Range Trajectory Height • Inches	0.0	0.1	0.6	1.5	2.9	4.8	7.4	10.6	14.5
Drop • Inches	0.0	-0.6	-2.4	-5.8	-10.7	-17.5	-26.3	-37.2	-50.5

Speer 100-grain GDHP (23913)

G1 Ballistic Coefficient = 0.160

Distance • Yards	Muzzle	25	50	75	100	125	150	175	200
Velocity • fps	1500	1408	1324	1248	1181	1124	1076	1036	1001
Energy • ft-lbs	500	440	389	346	310	280	257	238	223
Taylor KO Index	6.7	6.3	5.9	5.6	5.3	5.0	4.8	4.6	4.5
Mid-Range Trajectory Height • Inches	0.0	0.1	0.5	1.3	2.5	4.1	6.3	9.1	12.5
Drop • Inches	0.0	-0.5	-2.1	-4.9	-9.2	-15.0	-22.5	-31.9	-43.3

.357 Magnum

Magtech 95-grain SCHP (FD357A)

G1 Ballistic Coefficient = 0.140

Distance • Yards	Muzzle	25	50	75	100	125	150	175	200
Velocity • fps	1411	1315	1230	1157	1097	1048	1007	972	941
Energy • ft-lbs	420	365	319	283	254	232	214	199	187
Taylor KO Index	6.9	6.4	6.0	5.6	5.3	5.1	4.9	4.7	4.6
Mid-Range Trajectory Height • Inches	0.0	0.1	0.6	1.5	2.9	4.7	7.3	10.4	14.3
Drop • Inches	0.0	-0.6	-2.4	-5.7	-10.6	-17.2	-25.9	-36.7	-49.8

Cor-Bon 100-grain Pow'RBall (PB357100/20)

G1 Ballistic Coefficient = 0.090

Distance • Yards	Muzzle	25	50	75	100	125	150	175	200
Velocity • fps	1450	1299	1175	1082	1013	959	914	875	840
Energy • ft-lbs	467	375	307	260	228	204	186	170	157
Taylor KO Index	7.4	6.6	6.0	5.5	5.2	4.9	4.7	4.5	4.3
Mid-Range Trajectory Height • Inches	0.0	0.1	0.6	1.6	3.1	5.3	8.3	12.1	16.8
Drop • Inches	0.0	-0.6	-2.4	-5.8	-11.1	-18.5	-28.2	-40.6	-55.8

Federal 100-grain Barnes Expander (P357XB1) ☺

G1 Ballistic Coefficient = 0.178

Distance • Yards	Muzzle	25	50	75	100	125	150	175	200
Velocity • fps	1400	1330	1260	1200	1140	1095	1055	1022	992
Energy • ft-lbs	610	545	490	445	405	373	346	325	306
Taylor KO Index	10.0	9.5	9.0	8.6	8.2	7.8	7.6	7.3	7.0
Mid-Range Trajectory Height • Inches	0.0	0.1	0.6	1.4	2.7	4.5	6.8	9.7	13.3
Drop • Inches	0.0	-0.6	-2.4	-5.6	-10.3	-16.7	-24.9	-35.0	-47.2

Fiocchi 125-grain SJSP (357C)

G1 Ballistic Coefficient = 0.202

Distance • Yards	Muzzle	25	50	75	100	125	150	175	200
Velocity • fps	1500	1426	1357	1293	1235	1182	1136	1095	1060
Energy • ft-lbs	625	565	511	464	423	388	358	333	312
Taylor KO Index	9.6	9.1	8.7	8.3	7.9	7.6	7.3	7.0	6.8
Mid-Range Trajectory Height • Inches	0.0	0.1	0.5	1.2	2.3	3.8	5.8	8.3	11.4
Drop • Inches	0.0	-0.5	-2.1	-4.8	-8.9	-14.3	-21.4	-30.1	-40.6

Hornady 125-grain FTX (90500)

G1 Ballistic Coefficient = 0.144

Distance • Yards	Muzzle	25	50	75	100	125	150	175	200
Velocity • fps	1500	1398	1301	1224	1153	1096	1048	1008	974
Energy • ft-lbs	624	543	470	416	370	334	305	282	263
Taylor KO Index	9.6	8.9	8.3	7.8	7.4	7.0	6.7	6.4	6.2
Mid-Range Trajectory Height • Inches	0.0	0.1	0.5	1.3	2.5	4.2	6.5	9.4	13.0
Drop • Inches	0.0	-0.5	-2.1	-5.0	-9.4	-15.3	-23.1	-32.9	-44.8

Fiocchi 125-grain SJHP (357D

G1 Ballistic Coefficient = 0.190

Distance • Yards	Muzzle	25	50	75	100	125	150	175	200
Velocity • fps	1450	1375	1306	1243	1187	1137	1095	1058	1026
Energy • ft-lbs	584	525	474	429	391	359	333	311	292
Taylor KO Index	9.3	8.8	8.3	7.9	7.6	7.3	7.0	6.8	6.6
Mid-Range Trajectory Height • Inches	0.0	0.1	0.5	1.3	2.5	4.1	6.3	9.0	12.3
Drop • Inches	0.0	-0.5	-2.2	-5.2	-9.5	-15.4	-23.0	-32.4	-43.8

Magtech 125-grain GDHP (GG357A)

G1 Ballistic Coefficient = 0.163

Distance • Yards	Muzzle	25	50	75	100	125	150	175	200
Velocity • fps	1378	1298	1221	1163	1110	1065	1027	994	965
Energy • ft-lbs	527	468	417	376	342	315	293	274	259
Taylor KO Index	8.8	8.3	7.8	7.4	7.1	6.8	6.6	6.4	6.2
Mid-Range Trajectory Height • Inches	0.0	0.1	0.6	1.5	2.9	4.7	7.2	10.2	14.0
Drop • Inches	0.0	-0.6	-2.5	-5.8	-10.8	-17.4	-26.1	-36.7	-49.6

Blazer (CCI) 158-grain JHP (5207)

G1 Ballistic Coefficient = 0.168

Distance • Yards	Muzzle	25	50	75	100	125	150	175	200
Velocity • fps	1250	1186	1130	1084	1044	1010	980	953	929
Energy • ft-lbs	548	493	448	412	382	358	337	319	303
Taylor KO Index	10.1	9.6	9.1	8.8	8.4	8.2	7.9	7.7	7.5
Mid-Range Trajectory Height • Inches	0.0	0.2	0.7	1.8	3.4	5.4	8.3	11.6	15.8
Drop • Inches	0.0	-0.7	-3.0	-7.0	-12.8	-20.6	-30.5	-42.7	-57.3

Fiocchi 158-grain Hornady XTP/JHP (357XTP)

G1 Ballistic Coefficient = 0.206

Distance • Yards	Muzzle	25	50	75	100	125	150	175	200
Velocity • fps	1250	1197	1149	1109	1072	1041	1013	988	966
Energy • ft-lbs	548	503	463	431	403	380	360	343	327
Taylor KO Index	10.1	9.7	9.3	9.0	8.7	8.4	8.2	8.0	7.8
Mid-Range Trajectory Height • Inches	0.0	0.1	0.7	1.7	3.3	5.3	7.9	11.0	15.0
Drop • Inches	0.0	-0.7	-3.0	-6.8	-12.5	-20.0	-29.5	-41.2	-55.0

Speer 158-grain GDHP (23960)

G1 Ballistic Coefficient = 0.168

Distance • Yards	Muzzle	25	50	75	100	125	150	175	200
Velocity • fps	1235	1173	1119	1074	1036	1003	974	948	924
Energy • ft-lbs	535	483	440	405	377	353	333	315	299
Taylor KO Index	10.0	9.5	9.0	8.7	8.4	8.1	7.9	7.7	7.5
Mid-Range Trajectory Height • Inches	0.0	0.1	0.7	1.8	3.4	5.6	8.4	11.8	16.1
Drop • Inches	0.0	-0.7	-3.0	-7.1	-13.0	-31.0	-31.1	-43.5	-58.3

Magtech 158-grain LFN (357L)

G1 Ballistic Coefficient = 0.138

Distance • Yards	Muzzle	25	50	75	100	125	150	175	200
Velocity • fps	1085	1037	997	963	933	905	880	856	834
Energy • ft-lbs	413	378	349	325	305	287	272	257	244
Taylor KO Index	8.8	8.4	8.1	7.8	7.5	7.3	7.1	6.9	6.7
Mid-Range Trajectory Height • Inches	0.0	0.2	1.0	2.3	4.3	7.0	10.5	14.6	20.0
Drop • Inches	0.0	-1.0	-3.9	-9.1	-16.6	-26.6	-39.2	-54.6	-73.1

Federal 180-grain Swift A-Frame (P357SA)

G1 Ballistic Coefficient = 0.185

Distance • Yards	Muzzle	25	50	75	100	125	150	175	200
Velocity • fps	1130	1090	1050	1020	990	965	942	920	900
Energy • ft-lbs	510	470	440	415	390	372	355	339	324
Taylor KO Index	10.4	10.0	9.7	9.4	9.1	8.9	8.7	8.5	8.3
Mid-Range Trajectory Height • Inches	0.0	0.2	0.9	2.1	3.9	6.3	9.4	13.0	17.7
Drop • Inches	0.0	-0.9	-3.6	-8.3	-15.0	-24.0	-35.3	-49.1	-65.4

Federal 180-grain JHP (C357G)

G1 Ballistic Coefficient = 0.205

Distance • Yards	Muzzle	25	50	75	100	125	150	175	200
Velocity • fps	1080	1050	1020	1000	970	948	929	910	893
Energy • ft-lbs	465	440	415	395	380	360	345	331	319
Taylor KO Index	9.9	9.7	9.4	9.2	8.9	8.7	8.6	8.4	8.2
Mid-Range Trajectory Height • Inches	0.0	0.2	0.9	2.3	4.2	6.7	9.9	13.6	18.4
Drop • Inches	0.0	-1.0	-3.9	-8.9	-16.1	-25.7	-37.6	-52.1	-69.2

.357 SIG

Fiocchi 100-grain Frangible Sinterfire (357SGFN) ☺

G1 Ballistic Coefficient = 0.125

Distance • Yards	Muzzle	25	50	75	100	125	150	175	200
Velocity • fps	1500	1384	1280	1191	1117	1059	1011	972	937
Energy • ft-lbs	499	425	363	315	277	249	227	210	195
Taylor KO Index	7.7	7.1	6.5	6.1	5.7	5.4	5.2	5.0	4.8
Mid-Range Trajectory Height • Inches	0.0	0.1	0.5	1.3	2.6	4.5	6.9	10.0	13.9
Drop • Inches	0.0	-0.5	-2.2	-5.1	-9.6	-15.9	-24.0	-34.4	-47.0

Fiocchi 124-grain Hornady XTP/JHP (357SGXTP)

G1 Ballistic Coefficient = 0.177

Distance • Yards	Muzzle	25	50	75	100	125	150	175	200
Velocity • fps	1400	1324	1255	1193	1139	1093	1054	1020	991
Energy • ft-lbs	540	483	434	392	358	329	306	287	270
Taylor KO Index	8.9	8.4	8.0	7.6	7.2	6.9	6.7	6.5	6.3
Mid-Range Trajectory Height • Inches	0.0	0.1	0.6	1.4	2.7	4.5	6.8	9.8	13.4
Drop • Inches	0.0	-0.6	-2.4	-5.6	-10.3	-16.7	-24.9	-35.1	-47.3

Fiocchi 124-grain FMJ (357SIGAP)

G1 Ballistic Coefficient = 0.152

Distance • Yards	Muzzle	25	50	75	100	125	150	175	200
Velocity • fps	1350	1267	1194	1132	1080	1038	1001	969	941
Energy • ft-lbs	505	442	395	353	324	297	276	259	244
Taylor KO Index	8.6	8.0	7.6	7.2	6.8	6.6	6.3	6.1	6.0
Mid-Range Trajectory Height • Inches	0.0	0.1	0.6	1.6	3.0	5.0	7.6	10.8	14.8
Drop • Inches	0.0	-0.6	-2.6	-6.1	-11.3	-18.3	-27.4	-38.6	-52.2

Speer 125-grain GDHP (23913)

G1 Ballistic Coefficient = 0.141

Distance • Yards	Muzzle	25	50	75	100	125	150	175	200
Velocity • fps	1350	1261	1184	1119	1066	1023	986	953	925
Energy • ft-lbs	506	442	389	348	316	290	270	252	237
Taylor KO Index	8.6	8.1	7.6	7.2	6.8	6.5	6.3	6.1	5.9
Mid-Range Trajectory Height • Inches	0.0	0.1	0.6	1.6	3.1	5.1	7.8	11.1	15.2
Drop • Inches	0.0	-0.6	-2.6	-6.2	-11.4	-18.6	-27.9	-39.4	-69.6

.380 Auto (9mm Browning Short)

Magtech 77-grain SCHP (FD380A)

G1 Ballistic Coefficient = 0.114

Distance • Yards	Muzzle	25	50	75	100	125	150	175	200
Velocity • fps	1099	1039	991	951	916	885	856	830	805
Energy • ft-lbs	207	185	168	155	144	134	125	118	111
Taylor KO Index	4.3	4.1	3.9	3.7	3.6	3.5	3.4	3.3	3.2
Mid-Range Trajectory Height • Inches	0.0	0.2	1.0	2.3	4.4	7.2	10.8	15.3	20.7
Drop • Inches	0.0	-0.9	-3.9	-9.0	-16.6	-26.7	-39.6	-55.5	-76.6

Magtech 85-grain GGJHP (GG380A)

G1 Ballistic Coefficient = 0.111

Distance • Yards	Muzzle	25	50	75	100	125	150	175	200
Velocity • fps	1082	1025	978	939	904	873	845	818	794
Energy • ft-lbs	221	198	181	166	154	144	135	126	119
Taylor KO Index	4.7	4.4	4.2	4.1	3.9	3.8	3.7	3.5	3.4
Mid-Range Trajectory Height • Inches	0.0	0.2	1.0	2.4	4.5	7.4	11.1	15.7	21.3
Drop • Inches	0.0	-1.0	-4.0	-9.3	-17.1	-27.5	-40.8	-57.1	-76.6

Hornady 90-grain FTX (90080)

G1 Ballistic Coefficient = 0.100

Distance • Yards	Muzzle	25	50	75	100	125	150	175	200
Velocity • fps	1000	953	913	878	846	817	790	764	740
Energy • ft-lbs	200	182	167	154	143	133	125	117	109
Taylor KO Index	4.6	4.4	4.2	4.0	3.9	3.8	3.6	3.5	3.4
Mid-Range Trajectory Height • Inches	0.0	0.2	1.2	2.8	5.2	8.5	12.7	17.9	24.3
Drop • Inches	0.0	-1.1	-4.6	-10.8	-19.7	-31.6	-46.9	-65.6	-88.0

Speer 90-grain GDHP (23606)

G1 Ballistic Coefficient = 0.101

Distance • Yards	Muzzle	25	50	75	100	125	150	175	200
Velocity • fps	990	945	907	873	842	813	786	761	737
Energy • ft-lbs	196	179	164	152	142	132	124	116	109
Taylor KO Index	4.5	4.3	4.2	4.0	3.9	3.7	3.6	3.5	3.4
Mid-Range Trajectory Height • Inches	0.0	0.3	1.2	2.8	5.3	8.6	12.8	18.2	24.6
Drop • Inches	0.0	-1.1	-4.7	-10.9	-20.0	-32.1	-47.6	-66.5	-89.2

Aguila 90-grain JHP (1E802112)

G1 Ballistic Coefficient = 0.100

Distance • Yards	Muzzle	25	50	75	100	125	150	175	200
Velocity • fps	945	906	872	840	812	785	759	735	712
Energy • ft-lbs	179	164	152	141	132	123	115	108	101
Taylor KO Index	4.3	4.2	4.0	3.9	3.7	3.6	3.5	3.4	3.3
Mid-Range Trajectory Height • Inches	0.0	0.3	1.3	3.1	5.7	9.3	13.8	18.3	26.5
Drop • Inches	0.0	-1.2	-5.2	-11.9	-21.7	-34.9	-51.8	-71.9	-96.4

Magtech 95-grain JHP (380B)

G1 Ballistic Coefficient = 0.116

Distance • Yards	Muzzle	25	50	75	100	125	150	175	200
Velocity • fps	951	917	886	858	832	807	784	762	741
Energy • ft-lbs	191	177	166	155	146	137	130	122	116
Taylor KO Index	4.6	4.4	4.3	4.2	4.0	3.9	3.8	3.7	3.6
Mid-Range Trajectory Height • Inches	0.0	0.3	1.3	3.0	5.5	8.9	13.3	18.7	25.2
Drop • Inches	0.0	-1.2	-5.0	-11.6	-21.2	-33.8	-49.9	-69.4	-92.7

Blazer (CCI) 95-grain FMJ RN (5202)

G1 Ballistic Coefficient = 0.131

Distance • Yards	Muzzle	25	50	75	100	125	150	175	200
Velocity • fps	945	915	888	862	839	817	796	776	757
Energy • ft-lbs	188	177	166	157	149	141	134	127	121
Taylor KO Index	4.6	4.4	4.3	4.2	4.1	3.9	3.8	3.7	3.7
Mid-Range Trajectory Height • Inches	0.0	0.3	1.3	3.0	5.5	8.4	13.2	18.4	24.7
Drop • Inches	0.0	-1.2	-5.1	-11.7	-21.2	-33.8	-49.6	-68.9	-91.8

Black Hills 100-grain Full Metal Jacket (D380N3)

G1 Ballistic Coefficient = 0.125

Distance • Yards	Muzzle	25	50	75	100	125	150	175	200
Velocity • fps	950	918	889	863	838	815	793	772	752
Energy • ft-lbs	200	187	176	165	156	147	140	132	126
Taylor KO Index	4.8	4.7	4.5	4.4	4.3	4.2	4.0	3.9	3.8
Mid-Range Trajectory Height • Inches	0.0	0.3	1.3	3.0	5.5	8.8	13.1	18.4	24.8
Drop • Inches	0.0	-1.2	-5.0	-11.6	-21.1	-33.6	-49.5	-68.8	-91.7

9mm Makarov (9x18mm)

Sellier & Bellot 95-grain FMJ (V310912U)

G1 Ballistic Coefficient = 0.108

Distance • Yards	Muzzle	25	50	75	100	125	150	175	200
Velocity • fps	1017	971	931	897	866	837	810	786	762
Energy • ft-lbs	218	199	183	170	158	148	139	130	122
Taylor KO Index	4.9	4.7	4.5	4.3	4.2	4.1	3.9	3.8	3.7
Mid-Range Trajectory Height • Inches	0.0	0.2	1.1	2.7	5.0	8.1	12.1	17.2	23.2
Drop • Inches	0.0	-1.1	-4.5	-10.4	-19.0	-30.4	-45.0	-62.9	-84.4

9mm Luger (9mm Parabellum) (9x19mm)

Cor-Bon 80-grain Hornady DPX (DPX0980/20)

G1 Ballistic Coefficient = 0.165

Distance • Yards	Muzzle	25	50	75	100	125	150	175	200
Velocity • fps	1300	1241	1187	1140	1099	1063	1032	1004	979
Energy • ft-lbs	300	273	250	231	215	201	189	179	170
Taylor KO Index	5.3	5.0	4.8	4.6	4.5	4.3	4.2	4.1	4.0
Mid-Range Trajectory Height • Inches	0.0	0.1	0.7	1.6	3.1	5.0	7.5	10.6	14.4
Drop • Inches	0.0	-0.7	-2.7	-6.4	-11.6	-18.7	-27.7	-38.8	-52.0

Fiocchi 100-grain Frangible Non-Toxic (9SFNT) ☺

G1 Ballistic Coefficient = 0.111

Distance • Yards	Muzzle	25	50	75	100	125	150	175	200
Velocity • fps	1300	1197	1114	1050	999	956	920	888	858
Energy • ft-lbs	375	318	275	245	221	203	188	175	163
Taylor KO Index	6.6	6.1	5.7	5.3	5.1	4.9	4.7	4.5	4.4
Mid-Range Trajectory Height • Inches	0.0	0.1	0.7	1.8	3.5	5.8	8.8	12.7	17.4
Drop • Inches	0.0	-0.7	-2.9	-6.8	-12.7	-20.8	-31.3	-44.3	-60.1

Hornady 115-grain FTX (90250)

G1 Ballistic Coefficient = 0.130

Distance • Yards	Muzzle	25	50	75	100	125	150	175	200
Velocity • fps	1135	1075	1026	986	950	920	892	866	843
Energy • ft-lbs	329	295	269	248	231	216	203	192	181
Taylor KO Index	6.6	6.3	6.0	5.8	5.6	5.4	5.2	5.1	4.9
Mid-Range Trajectory Height • Inches	0.0	0.2	0.9	2.2	4.1	6.7	10.0	14.2	19.2
Drop • Inches	0.0	-0.9	-3.6	-8.4	-15.5	-24.9	-37.0	-51.7	-69.3

Black Hills 115-grain Barnes Tac-XP + P (D9N10) ☺

G1 Ballistic Coefficient = 0.150

Distance • Yards	Muzzle	25	50	75	100	125	150	175	200
Velocity • fps	1250	1179	1119	1069	1027	991	960	933	907
Energy • ft-lbs	400	355	320	292	269	251	236	222	210
Taylor KO Index	7.3	6.9	6.5	6.3	6.0	5.8	5.6	5.5	5.3
Mid-Range Trajectory Height • Inches	0.0	0.2	0.7	1.8	3.4	5.6	8.5	12.1	16.4
Drop • Inches	0.0	-0.7	-3.0	-7.0	-13.0	-20.9	-31.1	-43.7	-58.7

Blazer (CCI) 115-grain FMJ RN (5200)

G1 Ballistic Coefficient = 0.151

Distance • Yards	Muzzle	25	50	75	100	125	150	175	200
Velocity • fps	1145	1091	1046	1008	975	946	920	895	873
Energy • ft-lbs	335	304	278	259	247	229	216	205	195
Taylor KO Index	6.7	6.4	6.1	5.9	5.7	5.5	5.4	5.2	5.1
Mid-Range Trajectory Height • Inches	0.0	0.2	0.9	2.1	3.9	6.4	9.6	13.5	18.2
Drop • Inches	0.0	-0.9	-3.5	-8.2	-15.0	-24.1	-35.6	-49.7	-66.5

Aguila 117-grain JHP (1E092112)

G1 Ballistic Coefficient = 0.145

Distance • Yards	Muzzle	25	50	75	100	125	150	175	200
Velocity • fps	1250	1176	1115	1064	1022	986	954	926	901
Energy • ft-lbs	406	360	323	294	271	253	237	223	211
Taylor KO Index	7.4	7.0	6.6	6.3	6.1	5.9	5.7	5.5	5.4
Mid-Range Trajectory Height • Inches	0.0	0.2	0.7	1.8	3.5	5.7	8.6	12.2	16.6
Drop • Inches	0.0	-0.7	-3.0	-7.1	-13.0	-21.1	-31.3	-44.0	-59.2

Fiocchi 123-grain TC Enclosed Base, Leadless Primer (9TCEB123) ☺

G1 Ballistic Coefficient = 0.148

Distance • Yards	Muzzle	25	50	75	100	125	150	175	200
Velocity • fps	1180	1119	1068	1026	990	959	931	905	882
Energy • ft-lbs	383	345	314	290	270	253	239	226	214
Taylor KO Index	7.4	7.1	6.7	6.5	6.2	6.0	5.9	5.7	5.6
Mid-Range Trajectory Height • Inches	0.0	0.2	0.9	2.1	3.8	6.2	9.3	13.0	17.7
Drop • Inches	0.0	-0.8	-3.4	-7.8	-14.3	-23.0	-34.1	-47.7	-63.9

Winchester 124-grain Bonded PDX1 + P (S9MMPDB)

G1 Ballistic Coefficient = 0.170

Distance • Yards	Muzzle	25	50	75	100	125	150	175	200
Velocity • fps	1200	1143	1095	1054	1019	988	961	936	913
Energy • ft-lbs	396	360	330	306	286	269	254	241	230
Taylor KO Index	7.6	7.2	6.9	6.6	6.4	6.2	6.1	5.9	5.8
Mid-Range Trajectory Height • Inches	0.0	0.2	0.8	1.9	3.6	5.9	8.8	12.4	16.7
Drop • Inches	0.0	-0.8	-3.2	-7.5	-13.7	-22.0	-32.5	-45.4	-60.7

Fiocchi 124-grain Hornady XTP JHP (9XTPC

G1 Ballistic Coefficient = 0.165

Distance • Yards	Muzzle	25	50	75	100	125	150	175	200
Velocity • fps	1290	1220	1159	1107	1063	1025	993	964	939
Energy • ft-lbs	458	410	370	337	311	290	272	256	243
Taylor KO Index	8.1	7.7	7.3	7.0	6.7	6.5	6.3	6.1	5.9
Mid-Range Trajectory Height • Inches	0.0	0.1	0.7	1.7	3.2	5.3	7.9	11.3	15.3
Drop • Inches	0.0	-0.7	-2.8	-6.6	-12.1	-19.6	-29.1	-40.8	-54.8

Fiocchi 124-grain JHP (9APBHP

G1 Ballistic Coefficient = 0.165

Distance • Yards	Muzzle	25	50	75	100	125	150	175	200
Velocity • fps	1180	1125	1077	1038	1005	975	948	924	901
Energy • ft-lbs	383	348	319	297	278	262	247	235	224
Taylor KO Index	7.4	7.1	6.8	6.5	6.3	6.1	6.0	5.8	5.7
Mid-Range Trajectory Height • Inches	0.0	0.2	0.8	2.0	3.7	6.0	9.0	12.7	17.2
Drop • Inches	0.0	-0.8	-3.3	-7.7	-14.1	-22.7	-33.5	-46.8	-62.6

American Eagle (Federal) 124-grain Full Metal Jacket (AE9AP

G1 Ballistic Coefficient = 0.165

Distance • Yards	Muzzle	25	50	75	100	125	150	175	200
Velocity • fps	1150	1100	1050	1010	980	981	925	901	878
Energy • ft-lbs	365	330	305	280	265	249	235	223	212
Taylor KO Index	7.3	6.9	6.6	6.4	6.2	6.0	5.8	5.7	5.5
Mid-Range Trajectory Height • Inches	0.0	0.2	0.9	2.1	3.9	6.4	9.5	13.4	18.1
Drop • Inches	0.0	-0.8	-3.5	-8.1	-14.9	-23.9	-35.3	-49.2	-65.8

USA (Winchester) 124-grain Full Metal Jacket (USA9MM)

G1 Ballistic Coefficient = 0.205

Distance • Yards	Muzzle	25	50	75	100	125	150	175	200
Velocity • fps	1140	1091	1050	1015	984	957	932	909	888
Energy • ft-lbs	358	328	303	284	267	252	239	228	217
Taylor KO Index	7.2	6.9	6.6	6.4	6.2	6.0	5.9	5.7	5.6
Mid-Range Trajectory Height • Inches	0.0	0.2	0.9	2.1	3.9	6.3	9.4	13.3	17.9
Drop • Inches	0.0	-0.9	-3.6	-8.2	-15.0	-24.0	-35.3	-49.2	-65.7

Hornady 124-grain TAP-FPD (90248)

G1 Ballistic Coefficient = 0.173

Distance • Yards	Muzzle	25	50	75	100	125	150	175	200
Velocity • fps	1110	1067	1030	999	971	946	923	901	881
Energy • ft-lbs	339	314	292	275	260	246	235	224	214
Taylor KO Index	7.0	6.7	6.5	6.3	6.1	6.0	5.8	5.7	5.6
Mid-Range Trajectory Height • Inches	0.0	0.2	1.0	2.2	4.1	6.5	9.7	13.6	18.3
Drop • Inches	0.0	-0.9	-3.7	-8.6	-15.6	-24.9	-36.6	-50.9	-67.8

Blazer (CCI) 124-grain TMJ (3560)

G1 Ballistic Coefficient = 0.165

Distance • Yards	Muzzle	25	50	75	100	125	150	175	200
Velocity • fps	1090	1049	1014	982	955	930	907	886	866
Energy • ft-lbs	327	303	283	266	251	238	227	216	206
Taylor KO Index	6.9	6.6	6.4	6.2	6.0	5.9	5.7	5.6	5.5
Mid-Range Trajectory Height • Inches	0.0	0.2	1.0	2.3	4.2	6.8	10.1	14.2	19.0
Drop • Inches	0.0	-0.9	-3.8	-8.9	-16.2	-25.8	-38.0	-52.8	-70.4

Blazer (CCI) 124-grain FMJ RN (5201)

G1 Ballistic Coefficient = 0.165

Distance • Yards	Muzzle	25	50	75	100	125	150	175	200
Velocity • fps	1090	1049	1014	982	955	930	907	886	866
Energy • ft-lbs	327	303	283	266	251	238	227	216	206
Taylor KO Index	6.9	6.6	6.4	6.2	6.0	5.9	5.7	5.6	5.5
Mid-Range Trajectory Height • Inches	0.0	0.2	1.0	2.3	4.2	6.8	10.1	14.2	19.0
Drop • Inches	0.0	-0.9	-3.8	-8.9	-16.2	-25.8	-38.0	-52.8	-70.4

Winchester 147-grain Bonded PDX1 (S9MMPDB1)

G1 Ballistic Coefficient = 0.205

Distance • Yards	Muzzle	25	50	75	100	125	150	175	200
Velocity • fps	1000	976	954	934	915	897	881	865	849
Energy • ft-lbs	326	311	297	285	273	263	253	244	236
Taylor KO Index	7.5	7.3	7.1	7.0	6.8	6.7	6.6	6.5	6.3
Mid-Range Trajectory Height • Inches	0.0	0.2	1.1	2.6	4.7	7.6	11.2	15.5	20.7
Drop • Inches	0.0	-1.1	-4.5	-10.3	-18.5	-29.4	-42.9	-59.3	-78.5

Winchester 9x23mm

Cor-Bon 100-grain Pow'RBall (PB9X23100/20)

G1 Ballistic Coefficient = 0.100

Distance • Yards	Muzzle	25	50	75	100	125	150	175	200
Velocity • fps	1600	1445	1309	1194	1104	1036	983	936	901
Energy • ft-lbs	569	464	381	317	271	238	215	196	180
Taylor KO Index	8.2	7.4	6.7	6.1	5.6	5.3	5.0	4.8	4.6
Mid-Range Trajectory Height • Inches	0.0	0.1	0.5	1.3	2.5	4.4	6.9	10.2	14.2
Drop • Inches	0.0	-0.4	-2.0	-4.7	-9.0	-15.1	-23.2	-33.5	-46.3

.38 Super Auto Colt

Cor-Bon 100-grain Pow'RBall (PB38X100/20)

G1 Ballistic Coefficient = 0.100

Distance • Yards	Muzzle	25	50	75	100	125	150	175	200
Velocity • fps	1525	1379	1252	1149	1070	1009	961	920	884
Energy • ft-lbs	516	422	348	293	254	226	205	188	174
Taylor KO Index	7.8	7.1	6.4	5.9	5.5	5.2	4.9	4.7	4.5
Mid-Range Trajectory Height • Inches	0.0	0.1	0.5	1.4	2.7	4.7	7.4	10.8	15.1
Drop • Inches	0.0	-0.5	-2.2	-5.2	-9.9	-16.4	-25.1	-36.2	-49.8

USA (Winchester) 130-grain FMJ (Q4205)

G1 Ballistic Coefficient = 0.158

Distance • Yards	Muzzle	25	50	75	100	125	150	175	200
Velocity • fps	1215	1152	1099	1054	1017	984	955	929	906
Energy • ft-lbs	426	383	348	321	299	280	264	249	237
Taylor KO Index	8.1	7.7	7.3	7.0	6.8	6.5	6.3	6.2	6.0
Mid-Range Trajectory Height • Inches	0.0	0.2	0.8	1.9	3.6	5.8	8.7	12.4	16.9
Drop • Inches	0.0	-0.8	-3.2	-7.4	-13.5	-21.8	-32.2	-45.1	-60.5

.38 Special (.38 Smith & Wesson Special)

Hornady 110-grain FTX + P (90311)

G1 Ballistic Coefficient = 0.131

Distance • Yards	Muzzle	25	50	75	100	125	150	175	200
Velocity • fps	1090	1039	997	961	930	901	874	850	827
Energy • ft-lbs	290	264	243	226	211	198	187	177	167
Taylor KO Index	6.1	5.8	5.6	5.4	5.2	5.1	4.9	4.8	4.6
Mid-Range Trajectory Height • Inches	0.0	0.2	1.0	2.3	4.3	7.1	10.6	15.9	20.1
Drop • Inches	0.0	-1.0	-3.9	-9.0	-16.5	-26.6	-39.2	-54.8	-73.3

Hornady 110-grain FTX (90310)

G1 Ballistic Coefficient = 0.131

Distance • Yards	Muzzle	25	50	75	100	125	150	175	200
Velocity • fps	1010	972	940	910	883	858	835	813	792
Energy • ft-lbs	249	231	216	202	191	180	170	161	153
Taylor KO Index	5.7	5.5	5.3	5.1	5.0	4.8	4.7	4.6	4.4
Mid-Range Trajectory Height • Inches	0.0	0.2	1.1	2.6	4.9	7.9	11.8	16.6	22.3
Drop • Inches	0.0	-1.1	-4.5	-10.3	-18.8	-30.1	-44.3	-61.6	-82.2

Fiocchi 110-grain Hornady XTP JHP (38XTPB)

G1 Ballistic Coefficient = 0.131

Distance • Yards	Muzzle	25	50	75	100	125	150	175	200
Velocity • fps	1000	964	932	903	876	852	829	807	787
Energy • ft-lbs	244	227	212	199	188	177	168	159	151
Taylor KO Index	5.6	5.4	5.2	5.1	4.9	4.8	4.7	4.5	4.2
Mid-Range Trajectory Height • Inches	0.0	0.2	1.1	2.7	5.0	8.1	12.0	16.8	22.6
Drop • Inches	0.0	-1.1	-4.6	-10.5	-19.1	-30.6	-45.0	-62.6	-83.6

Fiocchi 125-grain SJHP (38F)

G1 Ballistic Coefficient = 0.204

Distance • Yards	Muzzle	25	50	75	100	125	150	175	200
Velocity • fps	940	921	902	885	869	853	839	824	810
Energy • ft-lbs	245	235	226	218	210	202	195	189	182
Taylor KO Index	6.0	5.9	5.8	5.6	5.5	5.4	5.3	5.3	5.2
Mid-Range Trajectory Height • Inches	0.0	0.3	1.3	2.9	5.3	8.5	12.4	17.3	23.0
Drop • Inches	0.0	-1.2	-5.1	-11.5	-20.8	-32.9	-48.0	-66.2	-87.6

Magtech 125-grain SJHP Flat (38D)

1 Ballistic Coefficient = 0.163

Distance • Yards	Muzzle	25	50	75	100	125	150	175	200
Velocity • fps	938	914	892	871	852	833	816	799	783
Energy • ft-lbs	244	232	221	211	202	193	185	177	170
Taylor KO Index	6.0	5.8	5.7	5.6	5.4	5.3	5.2	5.1	5.0
Mid-Range Trajectory Height • Inches	0.0	0.3	1.3	3.0	5.4	8.7	12.9	17.9	24.0
Drop • Inches	0.0	-1.3	-5.1	-11.7	-21.1	-33.6	-49.1	-68.0	-90.2

Magtech 125-grain SJHP + P (38H)

G1 Ballistic Coefficient = 0.149

Distance • Yards	Muzzle	25	50	75	100	125	150	175	200
Velocity • fps	890	868	847	827	808	789	772	755	739
Energy • ft-lbs	278	264	251	240	229	219	209	200	192
Taylor KO Index	7.2	7.0	6.8	6.7	6.5	6.4	6.2	6.1	6.0
Mid-Range Trajectory Height • Inches	0.0	0.3	1.4	3.3	6.0	9.7	14.3	19.9	26.7
Drop • Inches	0.0	-1.4	-5.7	-13.0	-23.5	-37.3	-54.6	-75.6	-100.3

Federal 125-grain NyClad HP (P38MA)

G1 Ballistic Coefficient = 0.050

Distance • Yards	Muzzle	25	50	75	100	125	150	175	200
Velocity • fps	830	780	730	680	640	602	566	531	499
Energy • ft-lbs	190	165	145	130	115	101	89	78	69
Taylor KO Index	5.3	5.0	4.7	4.3	4.1	3.8	3.6	3.4	3.2
Mid-Range Trajectory Height • Inches	0.0	0.4	1.8	4.3	8.2	13.8	21.3	31.0	43.4
Drop • Inches	0.0	-1.6	-6.9	-16.3	-30.4	-49.7	-75.1	-107.2	-147.1

American Eagle (Federal) 125-grain FMJ (AE38K)

G1 Ballistic Coefficient = 0.185

Distance • Yards	Muzzle	25	50	75	100	125	150	175	200
Velocity • fps	890	870	850	830	820	807	792	778	765
Energy • ft-lbs	230	220	210	200	195	181	174	168	162
Taylor KO Index	5.7	5.5	5.4	5.3	5.2	5.1	5.0	5.0	4.9
Mid-Range Trajectory Height • Inches	0.0	0.3	1.4	3.2	5.9	9.5	13.9	19.3	25.7
Drop • Inches	0.0	-1.4	-5.6	-12.9	-23.2	-36.7	-53.6	-73.9	-97.8

Blazer (CCI) 125-grain FMJ FN (5204)

G1 Ballistic Coefficient = 0.147

Distance • Yards	Muzzle	25	50	75	100	125	150	175	200
Velocity • fps	865	844	824	805	786	769	752	736	720
Energy • ft-lbs	208	198	188	180	172	164	157	150	144
Taylor KO Index	5.5	5.4	5.3	5.1	5.0	4.9	4.8	4.7	4.6
Mid-Range Trajectory Height • Inches	0.0	0.3	1.5	3.5	6.4	10.2	15.1	21.0	28.1
Drop • Inches	0.0	-1.5	-6.0	-13.7	-24.8	-39.4	-57.7	-79.8	-105.9

Aguila 130-grain FMJ (1E38222521)

G1 Ballistic Coefficient = 0.190

Distance • Yards	Muzzle	25	50	75	100	125	150	175	200
Velocity • fps	950	929	909	890	872	855	839	824	809
Energy • ft-lbs	261	249	238	229	220	211	203	196	189
Taylor KO Index	6.3	6.2	6.0	5.9	5.8	5.7	5.6	5.5	5.4
Mid-Range Trajectory Height • Inches	0.0	0.3	1.2	2.9	5.2	8.4	12.3	17.1	22.8
Drop • Inches	0.0	-1.2	-5.0	-11.3	-20.4	-32.4	-47.4	-65.4	-86.6

Black Hills 148-grain Match HBWC (D38N3)

G1 Ballistic Coefficient = 0.060

Distance • Yards	Muzzle	25	50	75	100	125	150	175	200
Velocity • fps	700	664	631	599	568	539	512	486	461
Energy • ft-lbs	161	145	131	118	106	96	86	78	70
Taylor KO Index	5.3	5.0	4.8	4.5	4.3	4.1	3.9	3.7	3.5
Mid-Range Trajectory Height • Inches	0.0	0.5	2.4	5.8	10.9	18.1	27.5	39.6	54.8
Drop • Inches	0.0	-2.3	-9.5	-22.2	-41.0	-66.4	-99.4	-140.6	-191.1

Sellier & Bellot 158-grain SP (V311082U)

G1 Ballistic Coefficient = 0.191

Distance • Yards	Muzzle	25	50	75	100	125	150	175	200
Velocity • fps	889	871	855	839	824	809	794	781	767
Energy • ft-lbs	277	266	256	247	238	229	221	214	207
Taylor KO Index	7.2	7.0	6.9	6.8	6.6	6.5	6.4	6.3	6.2
Mid-Range Trajectory Height • Inches	0.0	0.3	1.4	3.2	5.9	9.4	13.9	19.3	25.6
Drop • Inches	0.0	-1.4	-5.6	-12.9	-23.2	-36.7	-53.5	-73.8	-97.7

Fiocchi 158-grain LRN (38C)

G1 Ballistic Coefficient = 0.178

Distance • Yards	Muzzle	25	50	75	100	125	150	175	200
Velocity • fps	880	862	844	828	812	796	781	767	753
Energy • ft-lbs	271	261	250	240	231	222	214	206	199
Taylor KO Index	7.1	6.9	6.8	6.7	6.5	6.4	6.3	6.2	6.1
Mid-Range Trajectory Height • Inches	0.0	0.3	1.4	3.3	6.1	9.7	14.3	19.8	26.4
Drop • Inches	0.0	-1.4	-5.8	-13.2	-23.7	-37.6	-54.9	-75.7	-100.3

Magtech 158-grain LFN (38L)

G1 Ballistic Coefficient = 0.138

Distance • Yards	Muzzle	25	50	75	100	125	150	175	200
Velocity • fps	800	781	762	745	718	711	695	679	664
Energy • ft-lbs	225	214	204	195	186	177	169	162	155
Taylor KO Index	6.4	6.3	6.1	6.0	5.9	5.7	5.6	5.5	5.4
Mid-Range Trajectory Height • Inches	0.0	0.4	1.8	4.1	7.5	11.9	17.6	24.6	32.9
Drop • Inches	0.0	-1.7	-7.0	-16.0	-29.0	-46.0	-67.4	-93.2	-123.8

.40 Smith & Wesson

Fiocchi 125-grain Frangible Sinterfire (40SFNT) ☺

G1 Ballistic Coefficient = 0.120

Distance • Yards	Muzzle	25	50	75	100	125	150	175	200
Velocity • fps	1265	1175	1102	1045	998	959	924	894	866
Energy • ft-lbs	444	383	337	303	278	255	237	222	208
Taylor KO Index	9.3	8.6	8.1	7.7	7.3	7.0	6.8	6.5	6.3
Mid-Range Trajectory Height • Inches	0.0	0.2	0.8	1.9	3.5	5.9	8.9	12.7	17.4
Drop • Inches	0.0	-0.9	-3.6	-8.4	-15.3	-24.5	-36.2	-50.5	-67.2

PMC 125-grain Sinterfire Frangible (40F) ☺

G1 Ballistic Coefficient = 0.136

Distance • Yards	Muzzle	25	50	75	100	125	150	175	200
Velocity • fps	1250	1172	1107	1055	1012	975	943	914	888
Energy • ft-lbs	433	381	341	309	284	264	247	232	219
Taylor KO Index	9.2	8.6	8.1	7.7	7.4	7.1	6.9	6.7	6.5
Mid-Range Trajectory Height • Inches	0.0	0.2	0.8	1.9	3.5	5.8	8.7	12.4	16.9
Drop • Inches	0.0	-0.7	-3.0	-7.1	-13.1	-21.3	-31.7	-44.6	-60.1

Magtech 130-grain SCHP (FD40A)

G1 Ballistic Coefficient = 0.160

Distance • Yards	Muzzle	25	50	75	100	125	150	175	200
Velocity • fps	1190	1132	1082	1041	1006	975	947	922	899
Energy • ft-lbs	409	370	338	313	292	274	259	246	233
Taylor KO Index	9.1	8.6	8.2	7.9	7.7	7.4	7.2	7.0	6.8
Mid-Range Trajectory Height • Inches	0.0	0.2	0.8	2.0	3.7	6.0	9.0	12.7	17.1
Drop • Inches	0.0	-0.8	-3.3	-7.6	-14.0	-22.5	-33.2	-46.4	-62.0

Black Hills 140-grain Barnes Tac-XP (D40N6) ☺

G1 Ballistic Coefficient = 0.150

Distance • Yards	Muzzle	25	50	75	100	125	150	175	200
Velocity • fps	1150	1095	1049	1010	977	947	921	896	874
Energy • ft-lbs	411	373	342	317	297	279	264	250	237
Taylor KO Index	9.4	9.0	8.6	8.3	8.0	7.8	7.6	7.3	7.2
Mid-Range Trajectory Height • Inches	0.0	0.2	0.9	2.1	3.9	6.4	9.5	13.5	18.2
Drop • Inches	0.0	-0.8	-3.5	-8.2	-14.9	-24.0	-35.4	-49.4	-66.2

Magtech 155-grain JHP (40D)

G1 Ballistic Coefficient = 0.166

Distance • Yards	Muzzle	25	50	75	100	125	150	175	200
Velocity • fps	1205	1146	1096	1051	1018	987	959	934	911
Energy • ft-lbs	500	452	414	383	357	335	317	300	286
Taylor KO Index	10.9	10.4	10.0	9.6	9.2	9.0	8.7	8.5	8.3
Mid-Range Trajectory Height • Inches	0.0	0.2	0.8	1.9	3.6	5.9	8.8	12.4	16.7
Drop • Inches	0.0	-0.8	-3.2	-7.4	-13.6	-21.9	-32.4	-45.3	-60.6

Hornady 165-grain FTX (91340)

G1 Ballistic Coefficient = 0.155

Distance • Yards	Muzzle	25	50	75	100	125	150	175	200
Velocity • fps	1175	1115	1066	1025	990	959	931	906	882
Energy • ft-lbs	506	456	416	385	359	337	318	301	285
Taylor KO Index	11.4	10.8	10.3	9.9	9.6	9.3	9.0	8.8	8.5
Mid-Range Trajectory Height • Inches	0.0	0.2	0.8	2.0	3.8	6.2	9.3	13.1	17.7
Drop • Inches	0.0	-0.8	-3.4	-7.8	-14.4	-23.1	-34.3	-47.9	-64.2

Speer 165-grain TMJ FN Lawman (53955)

G1 Ballistic Coefficient = 0.135

Distance • Yards	Muzzle	25	50	75	100	125	150	175	200
Velocity • fps	1150	1089	1040	999	964	932	904	879	855
Energy • ft-lbs	484	435	396	365	340	318	300	283	268
Taylor KO Index	11.1	10.5	10.1	9.7	9.3	9.0	8.7	8.5	8.3
Mid-Range Trajectory Height • Inches	0.0	0.2	0.9	2.1	4.0	6.5	9.8	13.8	18.7
Drop • Inches	0.0	-0.8	-3.5	-8.2	-15.1	-24.3	-36.0	-50.4	-67.6

American Eagle (Federal) 165-grain Full Metal Jacket (AE40R3)

G1 Ballistic Coefficient = 0.155

Distance • Yards	Muzzle	25	50	75	100	125	150	175	200
Velocity • fps	1130	1080	1040	1000	970	942	917	894	872
Energy • ft-lbs	470	425	390	365	340	325	308	293	279
Taylor KO Index	10.9	10.4	10.1	9.7	9.4	9.1	8.9	8.6	8.4
Mid-Range Trajectory Height • Inches	0.0	0.2	0.9	2.2	4.0	6.5	9.7	13.7	18.4
Drop • Inches	0.0	-0.9	-3.6	-8.4	-15.3	-24.5	-36.2	-50.5	-67.2

Speer 165-grain TMJ FN Lawman – Clean Fire (53982)

G1 Ballistic Coefficient = 0.135

Distance • Yards	Muzzle	25	50	75	100	125	150	175	200
Velocity • fps	1050	1007	971	939	911	884	860	837	816
Energy • ft-lbs	404	372	345	323	304	286	271	257	244
Taylor KO Index	10.1	9.7	9.4	9.1	8.8	8.5	8.3	8.1	7.9
Mid-Range Trajectory Height • Inches	0.0	0.2	1.0	2.6	4.6	7.4	11.1	15.6	21.0
Drop • Inches	0.0	-1.0	-4.2	-9.6	-17.6	-28.1	-41.4	-57.7	-77.0

Fiocchi 165-grain FMJ TC (40SWF

G1 Ballistic Coefficient = 0.148

Distance • Yards	Muzzle	25	50	75	100	125	150	175	200
Velocity • fps	1020	985	954	927	901	878	856	836	816
Energy • ft-lbs	381	356	333	315	298	283	269	256	244
Taylor KO Index	9.6	9.3	9.0	8.7	8.5	8.3	8.1	7.9	7.7
Mid-Range Trajectory Height • Inches	0.0	0.3	1.1	2.6	4.8	7.7	11.4	15.8	21.4
Drop • Inches	0.0	-1.1	-4.4	-10.1	-18.3	-29.2	-42.9	-59.6	-79.4

Blazer (CCI) 180-grain FMJ (3591)

G1 Ballistic Coefficient = 0.144

Distance • Yards	Muzzle	25	50	75	100	125	150	175	200
Velocity • fps	1000	967	937	910	886	863	841	821	802
Energy • ft-lbs	400	374	351	331	313	298	283	269	257
Taylor KO Index	10.3	10.0	9.6	9.4	9.1	8.9	8.7	8.5	8.3
Mid-Range Trajectory Height • Inches	0.0	0.3	1.2	2.7	5.0	7.9	11.8	16.5	22.2
Drop • Inches	0.0	-1.1	-4.6	-10.5	-19.0	-30.3	-44.5	-61.8	-82.3

UMC (Remington) 180-grain FNEB (LL40SW5)

Ballistic Coefficient = 0.180

Distance • Yards	Muzzle	25	50	75	100	125	150	175	200
Velocity • fps	990	964	940	918	898	879	861	844	827
Energy • ft-lbs	392	371	353	337	322	309	296	285	274
Taylor KO Index	10.4	10.2	9.9	9.7	9.5	9.3	9.1	8.9	8.7
Mid-Range Trajectory Height • Inches	0.0	0.3	1.1	2.7	4.9	7.8	11.6	16.1	21.5
Drop • Inches	0.0	-1.1	-4.6	-10.5	-19.0	-30.2	-44.2	-61.1	-81.1

Sellier & Bellot 180-grain TFMJ (V311232U)

G1 Ballistic Coefficient = 0.152

Distance • Yards	Muzzle	25	50	75	100	125	150	175	200
Velocity • fps	968	940	914	891	869	848	818	810	792
Energy • ft-lbs	375	353	334	317	302	287	274	262	251
Taylor KO Index	10.2	9.9	9.6	9.4	9.2	8.9	8.7	8.5	8.3
Mid-Range Trajectory Height • Inches	0.0	0.3	1.2	2.8	5.2	6.3	12.3	17.2	23.0
Drop • Inches	0.0	-1.2	-4.8	-11.1	-20.0	-31.9	-46.8	-64.8	-86.2

Speer 200-grain TMJ FN Lawman – Clean Fire (53882)

G1 Ballistic Coefficient = 0.167

Distance • Yards	Muzzle	25	50	75	100	125	150	175	200
Velocity • fps	915	893	873	854	836	818	802	786	770
Energy • ft-lbs	372	355	339	324	310	298	286	274	264
Taylor KO Index	10.7	10.5	10.2	10.0	9.8	9.6	9.4	9.2	9.0
Mid-Range Trajectory Height • Inches	0.0	0.3	1.3	3.1	5.7	9.1	13.4	18.6	24.9
Drop • Inches	0.0	-1.3	-5.4	-12.2	-22.1	-35.1	-51.3	-70.9	-94.0

.41 Remington Magnum

Federal 210-grain Swift A-Frame (P41SA)

G1 Ballistic Coefficient = 0.186

Distance • Yards	Muzzle	25	50	75	100	125	150	175	200
Velocity • fps	1270	1210	1150	1110	1070	1036	1006	979	955
Energy • ft-lbs	750	680	620	570	530	500	472	447	425
Taylor KO Index	15.6	14.9	14.1	13.7	13.2	12.7	12.4	12.0	11.7
Mid-Range Trajectory Height • Inches	0.0	0.1	0.7	1.7	3.2	5.3	7.9	11.2	15.1
Drop • Inches	0.0	-0.7	-2.9	-6.7	-12.2	-19.7	-29.2	-40.8	-54.8

.44 Smith & Wesson Special

Cor-Bon 135-grain Glaser Safety Slug (03800/04000)

G1 Ballistic Coefficient = 0.125

Distance • Yards	Muzzle	25	50	75	100	125	150	175	200
Velocity • fps	1350	1251	1166	1098	1043	988	961	927	898
Energy • ft-lbs	546	469	408	361	326	299	277	258	242
Taylor KO Index	11.2	10.4	9.7	9.1	8.7	8.3	8.0	7.7	7.5
Mid-Range Trajectory Height • Inches	0.0	0.1	0.7	1.7	3.2	5.3	8.1	11.6	15.9
Drop • Inches	0.0	-0.6	-2.6	-6.3	-11.7	-19.1	-28.7	-40.6	-55.1

Federal 200-grain Semi-Wadcutter HP (C44SA

G1 Ballistic Coefficient = 0.147

Distance • Yards	Muzzle	25	50	75	100	125	150	175	200
Velocity • fps	870	850	830	810	790	773	756	739	723
Energy • ft-lbs	335	320	305	290	275	265	254	243	232
Taylor KO Index	10.7	10.5	10.2	10.0	9.8	9.5	9.3	9.1	8.9
Mid-Range Trajectory Height • Inches	0.0	0.3	1.5	3.4	6.3	10.1	14.9	20.8	27.8
Drop • Inches	0.0	-1.5	-5.9	-13.6	-24.5	-39.0	-57.0	-78.9	-104.8

Cowboy Action Loads

Magtech 200-grain LFN (44B)

G1 Ballistic Coefficient = 0.152

Distance • Yards	Muzzle	25	50	75	100	125	150	175	200
Velocity • fps	722	707	693	678	665	651	638	625	612
Energy • ft-lbs	232	222	213	204	196	188	181	173	167
Taylor KO Index	8.9	8.7	8.6	8.4	8.2	8.0	7.9	7.7	7.6
Mid-Range Trajectory Height • Inches	0.0	0.5	2.1	5.0	9.0	14.4	21.2	29.6	39.4
Drop • Inches	0.0	-2.1	-8.6	-19.6	-35.3	-55.9	-81.6	-112.7	-149.4

Magtech 240-grain LFN (44B)

G1 Ballistic Coefficient = 0.100

Distance • Yards	Muzzle	25	50	75	100	125	150	175	200
Velocity • fps	761	737	714	691	670	649	629	610	592
Energy • ft-lbs	309	289	271	255	239	225	211	199	187
Taylor KO Index	11.3	10.9	10.6	10.2	9.9	9.6	9.3	9.0	8.8
Mid-Range Trajectory Height • Inches	0.0	0.5	2.0	4.6	8.5	12.6	19.0	28.8	38.9
Drop • Inches	0.0	-1.9	-7.8	-18.0	-32.8	-52.3	-77.0	-107.3	-143.3

.44 Remington Magnum (Pistol Data)

Fiocchi 200-grain Hornady XTP JHP (44XTBP)

G1 Ballistic Coefficient = 0.170

Distance • Yards	Muzzle	25	50	75	100	125	150	175	200
Velocity • fps	1490	1404	1325	1253	1189	1134	1087	1047	1013
Energy • ft-lbs	986	876	780	697	628	571	525	487	456
Taylor KO Index	18.4	17.3	16.4	15.5	14.7	14.0	13.4	12.9	12.5
Mid-Range Trajectory Height • Inches	0.0	0.1	0.5	1.3	2.5	4.1	6.2	9.0	12.3
Drop • Inches	0.0	-0.5	-2.1	-5.0	-9.2	-15.0	-22.4	-31.7	-43.0

Fiocchi 200-grain SJHP (44B)

G1 Ballistic Coefficient = 0.170

Distance • Yards	Muzzle	25	50	75	100	125	150	175	200
Velocity • fps	1475	1390	1312	1241	1178	1125	1080	1041	1008
Energy • ft-lbs	968	858	764	685	617	563	518	481	451
Taylor KO Index	18.2	17.2	16.2	15.3	14.5	13.9	13.3	12.8	10.8
Mid-Range Trajectory Height • Inches	0.0	0.1	0.5	1.3	2.5	4.2	6.4	9.1	12.6
Drop • Inches	0.0	-0.5	-2.2	-5.1	-9.4	-15.3	-22.9	-32.3	-43.8

Magtech 200-grain SCHP (44D)

G1 Ballistic Coefficient = 0.220

Distance • Yards	Muzzle	25	50	75	100	125	150	175	200
Velocity • fps	1296	1242	1193	1149	1110	1076	1046	1020	996
Energy • ft-lbs	746	685	632	587	548	515	486	462	440
Taylor KO Index	16.0	15.3	14.7	14.2	13.7	13.3	12.9	12.6	12.3
Mid-Range Trajectory Height • Inches	0.0	0.1	0.7	1.6	3.0	4.9	7.4	10.4	14.1
Drop • Inches	0.0	-0.7	-2.7	-6.3	-11.6	-18.6	-27.5	-38.3	-51.3

Winchester 240-grain Dual Bond (S44RMDB)

G1 Ballistic Coefficient = 0.191

Distance • Yards	Muzzle	25	50	75	100	125	150	175	200
Velocity • fps	1300	1238	1183	1134	1092	1055	1024	996	971
Energy • ft-lbs	901	817	745	685	635	594	559	529	502
Taylor KO Index	19.3	18.3	17.5	16.8	16.2	15.6	15.2	14.8	14.4
Mid-Range Trajectory Height • Inches	0.0	0.1	0.7	1.6	3.1	5.0	7.6	10.7	14.5
Drop • Inches	0.0	-0.7	-2.8	-6.4	-11.7	-18.8	-28.0	-39.1	-52.5

Fiocchi 240-grain XTP HP (44XTP)

G1 Ballistic Coefficient = 0.205

Distance • Yards	Muzzle	25	50	75	100	125	150	175	200
Velocity • fps	1350	1288	1231	1180	1134	1095	1060	1030	1003
Energy • ft-lbs	971	884	807	742	686	639	599	566	537
Taylor KO Index	20.0	19.1	18.2	17.5	16.8	16.2	15.7	15.3	14.9
Mid-Range Trajectory Height • Inches	0.0	0.1	0.6	1.5	2.8	5.1	7.5	9.9	13.5
Drop • Inches	0.0	-0.6	-2.5	-5.9	-10.8	-17.4	-25.8	-36.2	-48.6

Fiocchi 240-grain JHP (44D)

G1 Ballistic Coefficient = 0.172

Distance • Yards	Muzzle	25	50	75	100	125	150	175	200
Velocity • fps	1330	1258	1195	1139	1092	1052	1017	987	960
Energy • ft-lbs	943	844	761	692	636	590	552	520	492
Taylor KO Index	19.7	18.6	17.7	16.9	16.2	15.6	15.1	14.6	14.2
Mid-Range Trajectory Height • Inches	0.0	0.1	0.7	1.6	3.0	5.0	7.5	10.7	14.5
Drop • Inches	0.0	-0.6	-2.6	-6.2	-11.4	-18.4	-27.4	-38.5	-51.8

American Eagle (Federal) 240-grain JHP (AE44A)

G1 Ballistic Coefficient = 0.176

Distance • Yards	Muzzle	25	50	75	100	125	150	175	200
Velocity • fps	1230	1170	1120	1070	1040	1008	979	954	930
Energy • ft-lbs	805	730	665	615	570	541	511	485	461
Taylor KO Index	18.2	17.3	16.6	15.8	15.4	14.9	14.5	14.1	13.8
Mid-Range Trajectory Height • Inches	0.0	0.2	0.8	1.8	3.4	5.6	8.4	11.9	16.0
Drop • Inches	0.0	-0.7	-3.1	-7.1	-13.0	-21.0	-31.1	-43.4	-58.1

Federal 240-grain JHP (C44A)

G1 Ballistic Coefficient = 0.176

Distance • Yards	Muzzle	25	50	75	100	125	150	175	200
Velocity • fps	1230	1170	1120	1070	1040	1008	979	954	930
Energy • ft-lbs	805	730	665	615	570	541	511	485	461
Taylor KO Index	18.2	17.3	16.6	15.8	15.4	14.9	14.5	14.1	13.8
Mid-Range Trajectory Height • Inches	0.0	0.2	0.8	1.8	3.4	5.6	8.4	11.9	16.0
Drop • Inches	0.0	-0.7	-3.1	-7.1	-13.0	-21.0	-31.1	-43.4	-58.1

Federal 280-grain Swift A-Frame (P44SA)

G1 Ballistic Coefficient = 0.142

Distance • Yards	Muzzle	25	50	75	100	125	150	175	200
Velocity • fps	1170	1110	1060	1010	980	948	920	895	871
Energy • ft-lbs	850	760	695	640	595	559	527	498	472
Taylor KO Index	20.2	19.2	18.3	17.5	16.9	16.4	15.9	15.5	15.1
Mid-Range Trajectory Height • Inches	0.0	0.2	0.9	2.1	3.9	6.3	9.4	13.3	18.1
Drop • Inches	0.0	-0.8	-3.4	-8.0	-14.6	-23.5	-34.8	-48.7	-65.3

.45 G.A.P. (Glock Automatic Pistol)

Magtech 185-grain JHP (GG45GA)

G1 Ballistic Coefficient = 0.192

Distance • Yards	Muzzle	25	50	75	100	125	150	175	200
Velocity • fps	1148	1104	1066	1034	1005	979	955	934	914
Energy • ft-lbs	542	501	467	439	415	394	375	358	343
Taylor KO Index	13.8	13.2	12.8	12.4	12.1	11.7	11.5	11.2	11.0
Mid-Range Trajectory Height • Inches	0.0	0.2	0.9	2.0	3.8	6.1	9.1	12.8	17.2
Drop • Inches	0.0	-0.8	-3.5	-8.0	-14.6	-23.3	-34.3	-47.7	-63.5

Speer 200-grain GDHP (23978)

G1 Ballistic Coefficient = 0.138

Distance • Yards	Muzzle	25	50	75	100	125	150	175	200
Velocity • fps	970	939	911	885	862	839	818	798	779
Energy • ft-lbs	418	392	369	348	330	313	297	283	269
Taylor KO Index	12.6	12.2	11.8	11.5	11.2	10.9	10.6	10.4	10.1
Mid-Range Trajectory Height • Inches	0.0	0.3	1.2	2.8	5.2	8.4	12.5	17.5	23.4
Drop • Inches	0.0	-1.2	-4.8	-11.1	-20.1	-32.1	-47.1	-65.4	-87.1

Magtech 230-grain JHP (GG45GA)

G1 Ballistic Coefficient = 0.188

Distance • Yards	Muzzle	25	50	75	100	125	150	175	200
Velocity • fps	1007	980	956	934	914	894	876	859	843
Energy • ft-lbs	518	491	467	446	426	409	392	377	363
Taylor KO Index	15.0	14.6	14.3	13.9	13.6	13.3	13.1	12.8	12.6
Mid-Range Trajectory Height • Inches	0.0	0.2	1.1	2.6	4.7	7.6	11.2	15.6	20.8
Drop • Inches	0.0	-1.1	-4.4	-10.2	-18.4	-29.2	-42.7	-59.1	-78.4

.45 Auto (.45 ACP)

Fiocchi 165-grain Frangible Sinterfire (45SFNT) ☺

G1 Ballistic Coefficient = 0.110

Distance • Yards	Muzzle	25	50	75	100	125	150	175	200
Velocity • fps	1125	1058	1004	961	923	891	860	833	807
Energy • ft-lbs	464	410	370	338	313	291	271	254	239
Taylor KO Index	12.0	11.3	10.7	10.3	9.9	9.5	9.2	8.9	8.6
Mid-Range Trajectory Height • Inches	0.0	0.2	0.9	2.3	4.3	7.0	10.6	15.0	20.4
Drop • Inches	0.0	-0.9	-3.7	-8.7	-16.1	-25.9	-38.6	-54.2	-72.8

Magtech 165-grain SCHP (FD45A)

G1 Ballistic Coefficient = 0.168

Distance • Yards	Muzzle	25	50	75	100	125	150	175	200
Velocity • fps	1100	1058	1022	991	963	937	914	893	873
Energy • ft-lbs	443	410	383	360	340	322	306	292	279
Taylor KO Index	11.8	11.3	10.9	10.6	10.3	10.0	9.8	9.6	9.3
Mid-Range Trajectory Height • Inches	0.0	0.2	0.9	2.2	4.1	6.7	9.9	13.9	18.7
Drop • Inches	0.0	-0.9	-3.8	-8.7	-15.9	-25.4	-37.4	-51.9	-69.2

Black Hills 185-grain Barnes TAC-XP + P (D45N7) ☺

G1 Ballistic Coefficient = 0.167

Distance • Yards	Muzzle	25	50	75	100	125	150	175	200
Velocity • fps	1000	971	945	921	899	878	859	841	823
Energy • ft-lbs	411	387	367	349	332	317	303	290	278
Taylor KO Index	12.0	11.7	11.3	11.1	10.8	10.5	10.3	10.1	9.9
Mid-Range Trajectory Height • Inches	0.0	0.3	1.1	2.6	4.8	7.8	11.5	16.1	21.5
Drop • Inches	0.0	-1.1	-4.5	-10.4	-18.8	-29.9	-43.8	-60.6	-80.5

Hornady 185-grain FTX (90900)

G1 Ballistic Coefficient = 0.140

Distance • Yards	Muzzle	25	50	75	100	125	150	175	200
Velocity • fps	900	875	853	831	811	791	773	755	738
Energy • ft-lbs	333	315	299	284	270	257	245	234	224
Taylor KO Index	10.6	10.3	10.1	9.8	9.6	9.3	9.1	8.9	8.7
Mid-Range Trajectory Height • Inches	0.0	0.3	1.4	3.2	6.0	9.6	14.1	19.8	26.5
Drop • Inches	0.0	-1.4	-5.6	-12.8	-23.1	-36.7	-53.8	-74.6	-99.1

Magtech 185-grain GGJHP (GG45A)

G1 Ballistic Coefficient = 0.147

Distance • Yards	Muzzle	25	50	75	100	125	150	175	200
Velocity • fps	1148	1092	1046	1007	973	944	917	892	869
Energy • ft-lbs	542	490	449	417	389	366	345	327	311
Taylor KO Index	13.8	13.1	12.6	12.1	11.7	11.3	11.0	10.7	10.4
Mid-Range Trajectory Height • Inches	0.0	0.2	0.9	2.1	3.9	6.4	9.6	13.6	18.3
Drop • Inches	0.0	-0.8	-3.5	-8.2	-15.0	-24.1	-35.6	-49.7	-66.6

Magtech 200-grain LSWC (45C)

G1 Ballistic Coefficient = 0.075

Distance • Yards	Muzzle	25	50	75	100	125	150	175	200
Velocity • fps	950	899	854	815	799	746	715	685	653
Energy • ft-lbs	401	359	324	295	270	247	227	209	192
Taylor KO Index	12.3	11.7	11.1	10.6	10.1	9.7	9.3	8.9	8.5
Mid-Range Trajectory Height • Inches	0.0	0.3	1.3	3.2	5.9	9.8	14.8	21.1	28.9
Drop • Inches	0.0	-1.2	-5.2	-12.1	-22.3	-36.1	-53.7	-75.7	-102.2

Magtech 230-grain Hornady GGJHP (GG45B)

G1 Ballistic Coefficient = 0.163

Distance • Yards	Muzzle	25	50	75	100	125	150	175	200
Velocity • fps	1007	977	949	925	902	880	860	842	824
Energy • ft-lbs	518	487	460	437	415	396	378	362	346
Taylor KO Index	15.0	14.6	14.2	13.8	13.5	13.1	12.8	12.6	12.3
Mid-Range Trajectory Height • Inches	0.0	0.2	1.1	2.6	4.8	7.7	11.4	16.0	21.4
Drop • Inches	0.0	-1.1	-4.5	-10.2	-18.6	-29.6	-43.4	-60.1	-79.9

Fiocchi 230-grain Hornady XTP JHP (45XTP)

G1 Ballistic Coefficient = 0.151

Distance • Yards	Muzzle	25	50	75	100	125	150	175	200
Velocity • fps	900	877	856	836	817	798	781	764	748
Energy • ft-lbs	414	393	374	357	341	326	311	298	286
Taylor KO Index	13.4	13.1	12.8	12.5	12.2	11.9	11.7	11.4	11.2
Mid-Range Trajectory Height • Inches	0.0	0.3	1.4	3.2	5.9	9.5	14.0	19.5	26.1
Drop • Inches	0.0	-1.4	-5.6	-12.7	-23.0	-36.5	-54.3	-73.9	-98.1

Fiocchi 230-grain FMJ (45A)

G1 Ballistic Coefficient = 0.205

Distance • Yards	Muzzle	25	50	75	100	125	150	175	200
Velocity • fps	860	845	830	816	803	790	777	765	753
Energy • ft-lbs	377	365	352	340	329	319	308	299	289
Taylor KO Index	12.8	12.6	12.4	12.2	12.0	11.8	11.6	11.4	11.2
Mid-Range Trajectory Height • Inches	0.0	0.3	1.5	3.4	6.3	10.0	14.6	20.3	27.0
Drop • Inches	0.0	-1.5	-6.0	-13.7	-24.6	-38.9	-56.7	-78.1	-103.2

Blazer (CCI) 230-grain Clean-Fire • Totally Metal Jacket (3570)

G1 Ballistic Coefficient = 0.153

Distance • Yards	Muzzle	25	50	75	100	125	150	175	200
Velocity • fps	845	826	807	790	773	756	740	725	710
Energy • ft-lbs	365	348	333	318	305	292	280	269	258
Taylor KO Index	12.5	12.3	12.0	11.7	11.5	11.2	11.0	10.8	10.5
Mid-Range Trajectory Height • Inches	0.0	0.4	1.6	3.7	6.7	10.6	15.7	21.6	29.2
Drop • Inches	0.0	-1.6	-6.3	-14.3	-25.9	-41.1	-60.1	-83.0	-110.1

Blazer (CCI) 230-grain FMJ (5230)

G1 Ballistic Coefficient = 0.154

Distance • Yards	Muzzle	25	50	75	100	125	150	175	200
Velocity • fps	830	811	794	777	760	744	729	714	700
Energy • ft-lbs	352	336	322	308	295	283	272	261	250
Taylor KO Index	12.4	12.1	11.8	11.6	11.3	11.1	10.9	10.7	10.4
Mid-Range Trajectory Height • Inches	0.0	0.4	1.6	3.8	6.9	11.0	16.2	22.5	30.1
Drop • Inches	0.0	-1.6	-6.5	-14.8	-26.8	-42.5	-62.1	-85.8	-113.8

Magtech 230-grain FMJ SWC (45B)

G1 Ballistic Coefficient = 0.160

Distance • Yards	Muzzle	25	50	75	100	125	150	175	200
Velocity • fps	780	764	749	734	719	705	691	678	665
Energy • ft-lbs	311	298	286	275	264	254	244	235	226
Taylor KO Index	11.6	11.4	11.2	10.9	10.7	10.5	10.3	10.1	9.9
Mid-Range Trajectory Height • Inches	0.0	0.4	1.8	4.2	7.7	12.3	18.1	25.2	33.6
Drop • Inches	0.0	-1.8	-7.3	-16.8	-30.2	-47.8	-69.8	-96.4	-127.7

.45 Colt (often called .45 Long Colt)

Hornady 225-grain FTX (92792)

G1 Ballistic Coefficient = 0.120

Distance • Yards	Muzzle	25	50	75	100	125	150	175	200
Velocity • fps	960	926	895	867	841	817	794	772	751
Energy • ft-lbs	460	428	400	376	354	333	315	298	282
Taylor KO Index	14.0	13.5	13.1	12.7	12.3	11.9	11.6	11.3	11.0
Mid-Range Trajectory Height • Inches	0.0	0.3	1.2	2.9	5.4	8.7	13.0	18.3	24.6
Drop • Inches	0.0	-1.2	-5.0	-11.4	-20.8	-33.2	-48.8	-68.0	-90.7

Federal 225-grain Jacketed Soft Point (AE45LC)

G1 Ballistic Coefficient = 0.196

Distance • Yards	Muzzle	25	50	75	100	125	150	175	200
Velocity • fps	860	840	830	810	800	787	774	761	748
Energy • ft-lbs	370	355	345	330	320	309	299	289	280
Taylor KO Index	12.5	12.3	12.1	11.8	11.7	11.5	11.3	11.1	10.9
Mid-Range Trajectory Height • Inches	0.0	0.3	1.5	3.5	6.3	10.0	14.7	20.4	27.1
Drop • Inches	0.0	-1.5	-6.0	-13.7	-24.7	-39.0	-56.9	-78.4	-103.7

Speer 250-grain GDHP (23984)

G1 Ballistic Coefficient = 0.165

Distance • Yards	Muzzle	25	50	75	100	125	150	175	200
Velocity • fps	750	735	721	707	694	681	668	358	644
Energy • ft-lbs	312	300	289	278	268	257	248	239	230
Taylor KO Index	12.2	11.9	11.7	11.5	11.3	11.0	10.8	10.7	10.4
Mid-Range Trajectory Height • Inches	0.0	0.5	2.0	4.6	8.3	13.3	19.5	27.1	36.1
Drop • Inches	0.0	-2.0	-7.9	-18.1	-32.6	-51.6	-75.2	-103.8	-137.2

.454 Casull

Magtech 225-grain SCHP (454C)

G1 Ballistic Coefficient = 0.230

Distance • Yards	Muzzle	25	50	75	100	125	150	175	200
Velocity • fps	1640	1569	1501	1437	1375	1318	1264	1215	1171
Energy • ft-lbs	1344	1230	1126	1031	945	868	799	738	685
Taylor KO Index	23.9	22.9	21.9	21.0	20.1	19.2	18.4	17.7	17.1
Mid-Range Trajectory Height • Inches	0.0	0.1	0.4	1.0	1.9	3.1	4.7	6.8	9.3
Drop • Inches	0.0	-0.4	-1.7	-4.0	-7.3	-11.8	-17.5	-24.6	-33.1

Magtech 240-grain SJSP (454D)

G1 Ballistic Coefficient = 0.246

Distance • Yards	Muzzle	25	50	75	100	125	150	175	200
Velocity • fps	1771	1700	1632	1566	1502	1442	1384	1330	1279
Energy • ft-lbs	1672	1541	1419	1307	1203	1108	1021	942	872
Taylor KO Index	27.6	26.5	25.4	24.4	23.4	22.4	21.5	20.7	19.9
Mid-Range Trajectory Height • Inches	0.0	0.0	0.3	0.8	1.6	2.6	4.0	5.7	7.8
Drop • Inches	0.0	-0.4	-1.5	-3.4	-6.2	-10.0	-14.8	-20.7	-27.9

Magtech 260-grain SJHP (454A)

G1 Ballistic Coefficient = 0.266

Distance • Yards	Muzzle	25	50	75	100	125	150	175	200
Velocity • fps	1800	1734	1669	1607	1547	1488	1433	1380	1330
Energy • ft-lbs	1871	1736	1609	1491	1381	1279	1186	1100	1021
Taylor KO Index	30.4	29.2	28.1	27.1	26.1	25.1	24.2	23.3	22.4
Mid-Range Trajectory Height • Inches	0.0	0.0	0.3	0.8	1.5	2.5	3.8	5.4	7.3
Drop • Inches	0.0	-0.3	-1.4	-3.3	-5.9	-9.5	-14.1	-19.8	-26.5

Magtech 260-grain FMJ Flat (454B)

G1 Ballistic Coefficient = 0.266

Distance • Yards	Muzzle	25	50	75	100	125	150	175	200
Velocity • fps	1800	1734	1669	1607	1547	1488	1433	1380	1330
Energy • ft-lbs	1871	1736	1609	1491	1381	1279	1186	1100	1021
Taylor KO Index	30.4	29.2	28.1	27.1	26.1	25.1	24.2	23.3	22.4
Mid-Range Trajectory Height • Inches	0.0	0.0	0.3	0.8	1.5	2.5	3.8	5.4	7.3
Drop • Inches	0.0	-0.3	-1.4	-3.3	-5.9	-9.5	-14.1	-19.8	-26.5

Winchester 260-grain Dual Bond (S454DB)

G1 Ballistic Coefficient = 0.176

Distance • Yards	Muzzle	25	50	75	100	125	150	175	200
Velocity • fps	1800	1700	1605	1515	1430	1352	1279	1215	1158
Energy • ft-lbs	1870	1670	1488	1326	1181	1055	945	852	774
Taylor KO Index	30.4	28.7	27.1	25.5	24.1	22.8	21.6	20.5	19.5
Mid-Range Trajectory Height • Inches	0.0	0.1	0.3	0.9	1.7	2.8	4.3	6.2	8.6
Drop • Inches	0.0	-0.4	-1.4	-3.4	-6.3	-10.2	-15.4	-21.8	-29.8

.50 Action Express

Speer 325-grain DCHP (3977)

G1 Ballistic Coefficient = 0.169

Distance • Yards	Muzzle	25	50	75	100	125	150	175	200
Velocity • fps	1450	1367	1291	1221	1162	1110	1067	1030	998
Energy • ft-lbs	1517	1348	1202	1077	974	889	821	765	718
Taylor KO Index	34.2	32.2	30.4	28.8	27.4	26.2	25.2	24.3	23.5
Mid-Range Trajectory Height • Inches	0.0	0.1	0.6	1.4	2.6	4.3	6.6	9.4	12.9
Drop • Inches	0.0	-0.5	-2.2	-5.2	-9.7	-15.8	-23.6	-33.4	-45.2

.500 Smith & Wesson Special

Cor-Bon 350-grain FMJ (HT500S350FMJ/12)

G1 Ballistic Coefficient = 0.150

Distance • Yards	Muzzle	25	50	75	100	125	150	175	200
Velocity • fps	1100	1053	1014	980	950	923	899	876	855
Energy • ft-lbs	941	862	799	747	702	663	628	596	568
Taylor KO Index	27.9	26.7	25.8	24.9	24.1	23.4	22.8	22.3	21.7
Mid-Range Trajectory Height • Inches	0.0	0.3	1.0	2.3	4.2	6.8	10.1	14.3	19.2
Drop • Inches	0.0	-0.9	-3.8	-8.8	-16.1	-25.7	-37.9	-52.8	-70.5

.500 Smith & Wesson Magnum

Cor-Bon 275-grain DPX (HT500SW275/20)

G1 Ballistic Coefficient = 0.140

Distance • Yards	Muzzle	25	50	75	100	125	150	175	200
Velocity • fps	1665	1548	1440	1341	1253	1176	1113	1061	1018
Energy • ft-lbs	1693	1465	1267	1099	959	845	756	687	633
Taylor KO Index	33.2	30.9	28.7	26.8	25.0	23.5	22.2	21.2	20.3
Mid-Range Trajectory Height • Inches	0.0	0.1	0.4	1.1	2.1	3.5	5.5	8.0	11.2
Drop • Inches	0.0	-0.4	-1.7	-4.1	-7.7	-12.6	-19.2	-27.4	-37.7

Hornady 300-grain FTX (9249)

G1 Ballistic Coefficient = 0.200

Distance • Yards	Muzzle	25	50	75	100	125	150	175	200
Velocity • fps	1950	1857	1767	1681	1598	1518	1443	1373	1307
Energy • ft-lbs	2533	2298	2080	1882	1700	1536	1388	1256	1139
Taylor KO Index	42.5	40.4	38.5	36.6	34.8	33.0	31.4	29.9	28.5
Mid-Range Trajectory Height • Inches	0.0	0.0	0.3	0.7	1.4	2.3	3.5	5.0	6.9
Drop • Inches	0.0	-0.3	-1.2	-2.8	-5.2	-8.5	-12.7	-17.9	-24.3

Magtech 240-grain SJSP (500B)

G1 Ballistic Coefficient = 0.197

Distance • Yards	Muzzle	25	50	75	100	125	150	175	200
Velocity • fps	1801	1712	1626	1544	1467	1394	1326	1263	1206
Energy • ft-lbs	2341	2115	1909	1722	1553	1402	1268	1151	1050
Taylor KO Index	42.5	40.4	38.4	36.4	34.6	32.9	31.3	29.8	28.4
Mid-Range Trajectory Height • Inches	0.0	0.0	0.3	0.9	1.6	2.7	4.1	5.9	8.1
Drop • Inches	0.0	-0.4	-1.4	-3.3	-6.2	-10.0	-15.0	-21.1	-28.7

Magtech 240-grain SJSP – Flat Light Recoil (500L)

G1 Ballistic Coefficient = 0.197

Distance • Yards	Muzzle	25	50	75	100	125	150	175	200
Velocity • fps	1378	1311	1250	1195	1146	1103	1066	1034	1006
Energy • ft-lbs	1371	1241	1127	1030	948	879	821	772	731
Taylor KO Index	32.5	30.9	29.5	28.2	27.0	26.0	25.1	24.4	23.7
Mid-Range Trajectory Height • Inches	0.0	0.1	0.6	1.5	2.8	4.5	6.8	9.7	13.2
Drop • Inches	0.0	-0.6	-2.4	-5.7	-10.5	-16.9	-25.1	-35.2	-47.4

Hornady 350-grain XTP MAG (9250)

G1 Ballistic Coefficient = 0.145

Distance • Yards	Muzzle	25	50	75	100	125	150	175	200
Velocity • fps	1700	1585	1478	1379	1289	1210	1143	1087	1041
Energy • ft-lbs	2246	1954	1697	1478	1291	1138	1015	919	842
Taylor KO Index	43.2	40.3	37.5	35.0	32.7	30.7	29.0	27.6	26.4
Mid-Range Trajectory Height • Inches	0.0	0.1	0.4	1.0	2.0	3.3	5.2	7.6	10.6
Drop • Inches	0.0	-0.4	-1.6	-3.9	-7.3	-12.0	-18.2	-26.1	-35.8

Magtech 400-grain SJSP (500A)

G1 Ballistic Coefficient = 0.242

Distance • Yards	Muzzle	25	50	75	100	125	150	175	200
Velocity • fps	1608	1542	1478	1418	1361	1307	1257	1211	1169
Energy • ft-lbs	2297	2112	1942	1786	1645	1517	1403	1302	1214
Taylor KO Index	46.7	44.8	42.9	41.2	39.5	37.9	36.5	35.2	33.9
Mid-Range Trajectory Height • Inches	0.0	0.1	0.4	1.0	2.0	3.2	4.9	6.9	9.4
Drop • Inches	0.0	-0.4	-1.8	-4.1	-7.5	-12.1	-18.0	-25.2	-34.0

Hornady 500-grain FT – XTP (9252)

G1 Ballistic Coefficient = 0.185

Distance • Yards	Muzzle	25	50	75	100	125	150	175	200
Velocity • fps	1300	1236	1179	1126	1087	1050	1018	990	964
Energy • ft-lbs	1876	1698	1543	1416	1310	1224	1151	1088	1033
Taylor KO Index	47.2	44.8	42.8	41.0	39.4	38.1	36.9	35.9	35.0
Mid-Range Trajectory Height • Inches	0.0	0.1	0.7	1.7	3.1	5.1	7.6	10.8	14.8
Drop • Inches	0.0	-0.7	-2.8	-6.4	-11.8	-18.9	-28.1	-39.4	-52.8

Data for Rimfire Ammunition

.17 Mach 2

Hornady 15.5-grain NTX (83176) ☺

G1 Ballistic Coefficient = 0.115

Distance • Yards	Muzzle	25	50	75	100	125	150	175	200
Velocity • fps	2050	1885	1729	1584	1450	1330	1225	1139	1071
Energy • ft-lbs	149	122	103	86	75	61	52	45	41
Path • Inches	-1.5	-0.1	+0.7	+0.8	0.0	-1.8	-4.9	-9.4	-15.6
Wind Drift • Inches	0.0	0.3	1.2	2.7	5.0	8.0	12.0	16.7	22.2

CCI 17-grain V-MAX (0048)

G1 Ballistic Coefficient = 0.128

Distance • Yards	Muzzle	25	50	75	100	125	150	175	200
Velocity • fps	2010	1863	1724	1594	1471	1360	1262	1178	1108
Energy • ft-lbs	152	131	112	96	82	70	60	52	46
Path • Inches	-1.5	-0.1	+0.7	+0.8	0.0	-1.8	-4.8	-9.1	-15.0
Wind Drift • Inches	0.0	0.2	1.0	2.4	4.5	7.3	10.8	15.1	20.0

.17 Hornady Magnum Rimfire (HMR)

Hornady 15.5-grain NTX (83171) ☺

G1 Ballistic Coefficient = 0.115

Distance • Yards	Muzzle	25	50	75	100	125	150	175	200
Velocity • fps	2525	2339	2161	1991	1829	1677	1535	1406	1291
Energy • ft-lbs	219	188	161	136	115	97	81	68	59
Path • Inches	-1.5	-0.5	+0.2	+0.4	0.0	-1.0	-2.8	-5.5	-9.4
Wind Drift • Inches	0.0	0.2	0.8	2.0	3.7	6.0	9.0	12.8	17.3

CCI 17-grain V-MAX (0049)

G1 Ballistic Coefficient = 0.128

Distance • Yards	Muzzle	25	50	75	100	125	150	175	200
Velocity • fps	2550	2382	2220	2064	1915	1773	1639	1514	1399
Energy • ft-lbs	245	214	186	161	138	119	101	87	74
Path • Inches	-1.5	-0.5	+0.1	+0.3	0.0	-0.9	-2.5	-5.0	-8.3
Wind Drift • Inches	0.0	0.2	0.7	1.7	3.2	5.2	7.8	11.0	14.8

CCI 17-grain TNT HP (0053)

G1 Ballistic Coefficient = 0.100

Distance • Yards	Muzzle	25	50	75	100	125	150	175	200
Velocity • fps	2550	2336	2132	1938	1758	1588	1435	1300	1187
Energy • ft-lbs	245	206	172	142	116	95	78	64	53
Path • Inches	-1.5	-0.4	+0.2	+0.4	0.0	-1.1	-3.1	-6.1	-10.4
Wind Drift • Inches	0.0	0.2	1.0	2.3	4.3	7.0	10.6	15.1	20.5

CCI 20-grain Game Point (0052)

G1 Ballistic Coefficient = 0.125

Distance • Yards	Muzzle	25	50	75	100	125	150	175	200
Velocity • fps	2375	2210	2051	1898	1754	1618	1492	1376	1274
Energy • ft-lbs	250	217	187	160	137	116	99	84	72
Path • Inches	-1.5	-0.4	+0.3	+0.4	0.0	-1.2	-3.1	-6.1	-10.2
Wind Drift • Inches	0.0	0.2	0.8	2.0	3.7	5.9	8.9	12.5	17.0

CCI 20-grain TMJ (0055)

G1 Ballistic Coefficient = 0.130

Distance • Yards	Muzzle	25	50	75	100	125	150	175	200
Velocity • fps	2375	2216	2063	1915	1776	1644	1520	1406	1304
Energy • ft-lbs	250	218	189	163	140	120	103	88	76
Path • Inches	-1.5	-0.4	+0.3	+0.4	0.0	-1.1	-3.1	-5.9	-9.9
Wind Drift • Inches	0.0	0.2	0.8	1.9	3.5	5.7	8.5	11.9	16.1

5mm Remington Rimfire Magnum

Aguila 30-grain Soli (1B222405)

G1 Ballistic Coefficient = 0.138

Distance • Yards	Muzzle	25	50	75	100	125	150	175	200
Velocity • fps	2300	2155	2014	1880	1752	1630	1516	1410	1314
Energy • ft-lbs	352	309	270	235	204	177	153	132	115
Path • Inches	-1.5	-0.4	+0.3	+0.5	0.0	-1.2	-3.2	-6.1	-10.2
Wind Drift • Inches	0.0	0.2	0.8	1.8	3.4	5.4	8.1	11.4	15.4

.22 Long

CCI 29-grain GLRN (0029)

G1 Ballistic Coefficient = 0.080

Distance • Yards	Muzzle	25	50	75	100	125	150	175	200
Velocity • fps	1215	1100	1019	958	908	865	827	792	760
Energy • ft-lbs	95	78	67	59	53	48	44	41	37
Path • Inches	-1.5	+1.9	+3.4	+2.9	0.0	-5.5	-14.0	-25.6	-40.6
Wind Drift • Inches	0.0	0.6	2.2	4.7	8.0	12.1	16.8	22.3	28.4

.22 Standard Velocity and Match Ammunition

Fiocchi 38-grain HP (22HPSUB)

G1 Ballistic Coefficient = 0.130

Distance • Yards	Muzzle	25	50	75	100	125	150	175	200
Velocity • fps	950	919	891	866	842	819	798	778	758
Energy • ft-lbs	76	71	67	63	60	57	54	51	49
Path • Inches	-1.5	+2.9	+4.7	+3.8	0.0	-6.9	-17.0	-30.5	-47.6
Wind Drift • Inches	0.0	0.2	0.9	2.1	3.6	5.6	8.1	10.9	14.2

Federal 40-grain Solid (UM22) (922A)

G1 Ballistic Coefficient = 0.093

Distance • Yards	Muzzle	25	50	75	100	125	150	175	200
Velocity • fps	1080	1013	960	917	880	845	814	785	757
Energy • ft-lbs	105	91	80	75	70	63	59	55	51
Path • Inches	-1.5	+2.3	+4.0	+3.3	0.0	-6.1	-15.2	-27.6	-43.5
Wind Drift • Inches	0.0	0.4	1.6	3.4	5.9	9.0	12.7	17.0	21.9

Fiocchi 40-grain Training (22MAXAC)

G1 Ballistic Coefficient = 0.150

Distance • Yards	Muzzle	25	50	75	100	125	150	175	200
Velocity • fps	1050	1011	978	948	921	897	874	853	833
Energy • ft-lbs	98	91	85	80	75	72	68	65	62
Path • Inches	-1.5	+2.2	+3.8	+3.1	0.0	-5.7	-14.0	-25.2	-39.4
Wind Drift • Inches	0.0	0.2	1.0	2.1	3.6	5.6	7.9	10.6	13.8

Fiocchi 40-grain Super Match (22SM300)

G1 Ballistic Coefficient = 0.130

Distance • Yards	Muzzle	25	50	75	100	125	150	175	200
Velocity • fps	980	946	915	888	862	839	817	795	775
Energy • ft-lbs	85	80	75	70	66	63	59	56	53
Path • Inches	-1.5	+2.7	+4.4	+3.6	0.0	-6.5	-16.1	-29.0	-45.3
Wind Drift • Inches	0.0	0.3	1.0	2.1	3.8	5.8	8.3	11.2	14.6

Fiocchi 40-grain Rapid Fire Pistol (22SM280)

G1 Ballistic Coefficient = 0.130

Distance • Yards	Muzzle	25	50	75	100	125	150	175	200
Velocity • fps	950	919	891	866	842	819	798	778	758
Energy • ft-lbs	80	75	71	67	63	60	57	54	51
Path • Inches	-1.5	+2.9	+4.7	+3.8	0.0	-6.9	-17.0	-30.5	-47.6
Wind Drift • Inches	0.0	0.2	0.9	2.1	3.6	5.6	8.1	10.9	14.2